HORRIBLE

D1579118

THE GROOVY
GREEKS
AND
THE ROTTEN
ROMANS

Terry Deary ✷ Martin Brown

MSCHOLASTIC

Scholastic Children's Books,
Euston House, 24 Eversholt Street,
London NW1 1DB, UK

A division of Scholastic Ltd
London ~ New York ~ Toronto ~ Sydney ~ Auckland
Mexico City ~ New Delhi ~ Hong Kong

Published in this edition by Scholastic Ltd, 2003
Cover illustration copyright © Martin Brown, 1997

The Groovy Greeks
First published in the UK by Scholastic Ltd, 1995
Text copyright © Terry Deary, 1995
Illustrations copyright © Martin Brown, 1995

The Rotten Romans
First published in the UK by Scholastic Ltd, 1994
Text copyright © Terry Deary, 1994
Illustrations copyright © Martin Brown, 1994

10 digit ISBN 0 439 97332 5
13 digit ISBN 978 0439 97332 8

Printed by Nørhaven Paperback A/S, Denmark

8 10 9

Contents

The Groovy Greeks

The Rotten Romans

THE GROOVY
GREEKS

For Jean Longstaff, with thanks.

INTRODUCTION

History can be horrible. And do you know who to blame?

ER... MR POPPLECRUMP, MY HISTORY TEACHER?

No, it's the Greeks!

BUT THE ANCIENT GREEKS ARE DEAD AREN'T THEY?

DUNNO. WAS IT IN THE NEWSPAPERS?

NAH, IT WAS YEARS AGO

WHAT? BEFORE MR POPPLECRUMP WAS BORN?

WELL MAYBE NOT *THAT* LONG AGO

The Greeks invented history about 2,500 years ago . . .

Inventing history is just one of the things we have to thank them for. They had the idea for plays, for the Olympic Games – even the camera . . .

Funny you should mention that. Here is a book on the groovy Greeks. A book that will tell you all the things that teacher doesn't tell you. The things you really want to know. The hilarious stories and the horror stories.

GROOVY GREEK TIMELINE

BC

1600 – 1200 First Greek civilizations, ruled by the mighty Mycenaean lords of Crete.

About 1180 The siege of Troy – Troy loses to the famous wooden horse trick.

About 1100 The state of Sparta starts.

776 First recorded Olympic games.

About 750 – 550 Greeks take to the seas and become great traders.

About 730 Greeks produce the first works of written poetry in the world. Groovy Homer is the most famous.

640 World's first roof tiles manufactured at Temple of Hera at Olympia.

About 600 Thales, the Greek scientist, announces that the entire earth is actually floating in water.

585 Scientist Thales predicts an eclipse of the sun.

About 550 First plays performed. King Croesus of Lydia has gold and silver coins made; the first coins with writing on them.

9

About 530 Peisistratus of Athens creates a library.

About 520 Alcmaeon of Croton finds out about the human body by cutting up dead ones – groovy, eh?

490 Persians invade Greece – beaten by Greeks at The Battle of Marathon.

486 The first comedy drama at Athens.

480 Xerxes of Persia attacks the Greeks. The battle of Thermopylae. Spartan heroes die.

460 Athens v Sparta and Persia.

431 – 404 Athens tries to get too bossy so the others fight the Peloponnesian War. Sparta becomes top dog.

430 Great Plague of Athens kills Athenian leader, Pericles, not to mention a quarter of all the Athenian people.

413 A defeat at Syracuse for the army of Athens followed by . . .

404 The Fall of Athens.

About 400 Greek army engineers invent the stomach bow – the first type of crossbow.

371 Spartans lose to new top dog, the Thebans.

336 Alexander the Great becomes king of Macedon when his dad is assassinated. In just ten years he conquers the old enemy, Persia.

330 Aristotle invents the 'camera obscura' – a sort of pinhole camera and the idea behind today's film and television – now that really was groovy!

323 Alexander the Great dies. His generals divide up his empire.

322 The end of democracy in Athens when the Macedons take over.

215 Archimedes invents war machines like the catapult – they keep the Romans out for three years.

213 Archimedes has mirrors set along the harbour walls – they dazzle the Romans and set fire to their boats. . . Romans delayed for a while but. . .

212 Here come the Romans.

146 Greece part of the Roman Empire.

AD

393 Romans abandon Olympic Games – they don't happen again for 1500 years.

THE GRUESOME GODS

Before the groovy Greeks came the mighty Mycenaean people, who ruled Greece. Their greatest palace was on the island of Crete – it was so posh the queen had the world's first flushing toilet. Then the palaces were wrecked and the Mycenaean way of life went too. No more flushing toilets. What went wrong? Was it. . .

- war and attack from outside
- earthquakes
- disease and plague
- drought and famine
- change of climate?

They've all been suggested by historians. But, like the disappearance of the dinosaurs, no one really knows for sure.

The *Dorian* people moved down into Greece. They forgot how to write so we don't know a lot about those days. Historians call them the *Dark* Ages.

So, without writing, the history was preserved in stories. And, as the years passed, the stories became wilder and more unlikely. Legends, in fact.

The Greeks loved horror stories best of all. One Greek writer said that Greek children should not be told stories like this one (just as grown-ups today say you should not watch certain horror films).

But this book is a Horrible History and this story has a PG rating.

Do *not* read this story if you suffer from nightmares – or at least read it with your eyes closed so you don't suffer the most gory bits.

YOU HAVE BEEN WARNED!

Bringing up baby

Cronos was the chief god. You'd think that would make him happy, but no. Somebody told him that one of his children would take his place.

'Can't have that,' Cronos complained. 'Here, Mrs Cronos, pass me that baby!'

'What for?'

'Never mind daft questions. Just pass me that baby.'

Mrs Cronos passed across their new-born child. 'Here! What you doin' of with that baby?' she cried.

'Eatin' it.'

'Eatin' it! You great greedy lummock. You've just had your tea. You can't be hungry again already.'

NEEDS SALT

'I'm not hungry,' the great god growled. 'Just there's this prophecy about one of my children taking my throne. No kid, no take-over, that's the way I look at it.'

'You don't want to go takin' no notice of them horry-scopes,' Mrs Cronos sighed.

'Don't pay to take chances is what I always say,' Cronos said smugly. 'Pass them indigestion tablets.'

Time passed, as time does, and Mrs Cronos had more baby gods. . . and Cronos ate every last one. Well, not the *very* last one. Mrs Cronos was getting fed up with his gruesome guzzling. 'I'll put a stop to his little game,' she smirked as she hid the new baby, Zeus, under her bed. She picked up a big rock, wrapped it in a baby blanket and dropped it in the cot.

In walked Cronos. 'Where is it?'

'In the cot.'

'Ugly little beggar, isn't he?' the head god said, squinting at the boulder.

'Takes after his father then,' Mrs Cronos mumbled.

'Crunchy as well,' her husband said, swallowing teeth.

'Probably cos he's *bolder* than the rest,' Mrs Cronos agreed.

Cronos sat down heavily on a royal couch. 'Ooooh! I think I've eaten someone who disagrees with me.'

'It's possible,' Mrs Cronos sniffed. 'A lot of people disagree with you, sweetheart.'

'Ooooh!' The god groaned and clutched his stomach. 'I think I'm going to be sick!'

'Not on the new carpet, my love. There's a bowl over there,' Mrs Cronos warned him.

Cronos gave a heavenly heave and threw up not just his stony snack, but all the other baby gods as well. 'Just goes to show,' Mrs Cronos smiled happily. 'You can't keep a good god down!'

HI DAD

And did the young gods grow up to overthrow their dreadful dad? What do you think?

Don't feel too sorry for Cronos. He'd killed his own father, Uranus, and scattered the bits into the oceans. Cronos and the old gods were driven out by Zeus and the new gods. These new gods were much more fun. They were really one big, unhappy family. Always arguing, fighting and doing nasty things to each other.

Zeus ruled the earth and the sky from his home on the top of mount Olympus. Of all the groovy gods, Zeus was the grooviest. In a competition he got the top job. When he wasn't flirting with human women he was frying somebody with a thunderbolt.

Zeus's brother, Poseidon, ruled the sea. A job for a real drip. Old Pos wasn't too happy with this because he was a bad loser. That's why he sulked and went stomping around, whipping up the seas with a fork and creating storms. What a stirrer!

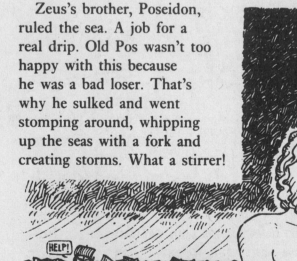

HELP!

16

A third brother, Hades, was the real loser. He won the job of ruling the underworld. That must have been hell!

Quick quiz

Prometheus, a young god, liked humans so he stole fire from the gods and gave it to men on earth. But top god, Zeus, punished men by creating something new and terrible on earth. What were these terrible things?

1 women
2 flies
3 teachers

Answer:

1 Women! The Greeks thought they were sly and lying. They attracted men so that men couldn't live without them — at the same time they were such a nuisance men couldn't live with them either. Women were a great help when it came to sharing a man's wealth but no help at all when he was poor. Of course this legend is utter nonsense — if you don't believe me then ask any woman.

17

FIGHT LIKE A GREEK

The wooden heads of Troy
Everybody knows the story of the wooden horse of Troy.
But can you believe it? Those Trojan twits saw a wooden
horse standing outside the gates of the city . . .

Everyone thinks it's a wonderful story. No one stops to ask, 'Would the Trojans really be that stupid?' But, if they *did* ask that question, the answer would have to be 'Yes.' If brains were gunpowder the Trojans wouldn't have had enough to blow their helmets off. Because they were tricked into letting the groovy Greeks into their city a *second* time.

That's right. Everyone knows about the wooden horse trick. Teachers forget to tell you about the *second* one over 800 years later in 360 BC. . .

Tricking a Trojan. . . again

Charidemus was fed up. He paced up and down in his tent and rubbed a strong hand through his greying hair. He complained, 'I'll never capture Troy. The walls are just too strong. . . and the Trojans don't look as if they're starving to death, do they?'

'No, sir,' his young lieutenant mumbled. 'Perhaps if we made a wooden horse and. . .'

Charidemus glared at him. 'Thank you. You are the fiftieth person to suggest that. The Trojans won't fall for that old trick again. Next time they'll just set fire to the wooden horse. Would you like to volunteer to sit inside it, eh? See if I'm right?'

The young man turned red and said, 'No, sir.'

He was relieved to hear someone approaching the tent. He jumped to the door.

'Password?'

'Ajax,' the man called.

The lieutenant opened the flap and said, 'Enter, friend.'

The guard stepped through, pulled on a short chain

20

and dragged a ragged man through after him. The guard stood to attention. 'Spy, sir. Caught him stealing food. Permission to execute him, sir?' he barked.

General Charidemus peered at the prisoner. The man's clothes were dusty but quite rich. 'Not yet, Captain. Leave us together.'

The guard saluted and strode out. Charidemus nodded to a cushion. 'Sit down,' he ordered. 'Your name?'

The prisoner grinned. 'Damon.' He was a wiry man with dark eyes that seemed to dart around and couldn't meet anyone else's gaze.

'And you've come out from Troy to steal our food? Are things that bad inside the city then?'

Damon smiled slyly. 'You Greeks eat better than the Trojans. Even before the siege the king gave us poor rations.'

'You don't like the king? Then why work for him?' the Greek general asked.

The prisoner shrugged. 'It's a job.'

Charidemus leaned forward. 'And if I offered you a job? A better paid and better fed job?'

Damon looked at his thumb and slowly placed it in his mouth. 'I'd be happy to work for you. I'd be loyal to you.'

The general's eyes were hard as iron as he replied, 'Oh, you'd be loyal, Damon. Men who betray me die... but they die very slowly.'

The prisoner squirmed on his cushion and gave a nervous smile. 'What do you want me to do?'

'I want you to be my wooden horse, Damon. Listen carefully and I'll tell you exactly what I want you to do . . .'.

It took a week for Charidemus to prepare the plan. His young lieutenant was nervous. As he tightened the buckle on his general's armour he asked, 'How do you know Damon won't betray us?'

The general tested the weight of his short sword. 'Damon is greedy but he's not stupid. He knows that we will take Troy sooner or later. If we have to wait too long to get inside he knows we'll be angry. We'll certainly kill the Trojan men – including him. But if he helps us he lives – and doesn't have to go to bed hungry any more.'

Charidemus slid the sword into his belt. 'Pass me my cloak.'

The young man took the large, filthy cloak and slid it over his general's wide shoulders. A hood covered the man's square head. He arranged the cloak to cover the weapons, dusted his hands and gave a nod. 'You'll pass as a poor traveller, sir.' The lieutenant changed too.

The general strode out of his tent and met a dozen men dressed the same way. No one spoke. Charidemus led the way from the torch-lit camp on to the stony road to Troy. A small man sat quietly on a horse and watched them approach.

'Is everything ready, Damon?' the general asked softly.

'It is,' the small man smiled. He turned his horse and walked slowly back towards the city gates. The Greek soldiers dragged their sandals and began to limp towards the enemy city.

'Who goes there?' a guard cried from a gate tower.

'Damon!' the traitor cried.

'Ah, so it is! What have you got with you?'

'The Greeks are growing careless. I went to their camp and found some of our captured men with just a single guard. I killed him and brought them back,' Damon lied. 'But let me in quickly. They're weak and sick!'

'Aye, Damon. . . oh, you'd better give the password.'

'Castor,' Damon said quickly.

The gates creaked slowly open. The man on the horse rode in – the soldiers trudged behind him.

As the gates closed the men stood in the shadow of the wall and shrugged off their cloaks. They climbed the stone stairways to the gate towers and the walls.

The Trojan defenders had no chance. They were looking for Greeks outside the walls – they didn't expect the attack to come from within.

Charidemus cut the throat of the last guard and let the limp body drop into the dark and dusty ditch that ran outside the wall. The Greeks gathered in the tower above the gate.

'Now we wait for the rest of our army. . .' the general began, but his lieutenant hurried to the walls and looked over. There was a rattle of stones on the road as a body of armed men arrived and halted.

'They're here, sir, but they're too early!' the young man gasped.

'Either that or they aren't *our* men,' Charidemus said.

'How can we tell in the darkness?'

'The password, man, the password . . . you know, "Wooden Horse". Quick! Challenge them,' the general ordered.

'Who goes there?' the lieutenant called.

'Friend!' came the reply.

'Give the password.'

After a moment a voice called, 'Castor!'

The Greeks looked at General Charidemus. 'Let them in. If we don't they'll raise the alarm before our men get here. Hide behind the gates. As soon as the last man is in, you come out. Kill them. Kill every last one!'

The Greeks trotted down the stairs to their positions while the general and his lieutenant turned the winches that opened the gates. There was the sound of marching feet, cries of surprise and fear, the clash of weapons, then the silence of death.

From the darkest shadow of the Trojan street a small man gave a grim smile as he sat astride his horse. A horse that had led the enemy into Troy . . . again.

PETRIFYING PLAYS AND ELECTRIFYING EPICS

After the stories of gods there were stories of heroes – men who were almost as powerful as gods. The only difference was they were 'mortal' – they could die.

The stories about heroes were told as poems. They were sung in the palaces of ancient Greece. Then, after the dark ages, poems were written down. The oldest written poem was by the Greek, Homer. His poem, *The Iliad*, tells the story of the siege of Troy, a story of the heroes who fought to the death to get Helen back to her hubby, King Menelaus.

It was such a great story it is still told today.

The Greeks heard the poems read on stage while a group of dancers performed. Then a clever poet called Aeschylus came along and had a great idea. He put a second reader on stage. Now you had a 'play' – the first drama in the world. Another groovy Greek invention!

Another famous playwright was Euripides – say 'you-rippa-deeze' – whose name gave lot of joy to suffering students of Greek.

Of course, like everything else in Greece, play-writing became a competition. You went to see which play was the best and would win the prize. But it wasn't like your local theatre where you can go and watch a pantomime at Christmas. Greek theatre. . .

- always had the same scenery
- was out in the open air
- had no actresses – only actors who also played the female parts
- had no action on stage – only people *talking about* the exciting bits – murders and all that happened off stage
- had the actors wearing face masks – and high platform shoes so they moved around very slowly

There were two types of play. Serious ones where lots of people died miserably – they were called 'tragedies'. Funny ones full of groovy jokes and rude bits – they were called 'comedies'.

Some of their favourite tragedies were about the Trojan War. Several writers told the same story. The skill was to tell it in an interesting way.

Playwright Aeschylus didn't write about the fighting at Troy – Homer's poem did that. Aeschylus looked at the story of the women left behind. Women like Clytemnestra – wife of the Greek leader, Agamemnon. If Clytemnestra had kept a diary of those exciting years, would it have looked like this . . . ?

Diary of a murder

Dear Diary,

You'll never believe what my sister Helen has gone and done! She's run off with that nice young man, Paris. She's a sly one that Helen. Husband Menelaus away from the palace and she chats up young Paris. Disgusting, I call it. You'd never catch me flirting with a guest. Of course I've got three kids to worry about. I have to set them a good example. Anyway, they reckon she's off to a place called Troy. Still, its better than Sparta. Nasty brutal place that Sparta. I always said she'd never stick it out.

TROY

There'll be trouble, mark my words. My husband, Agamemnon, came storming in tonight. 'Have you heard what your Helen's gone and done now?' he snaps.

'I've heard. Can't say I blame her. Nice young chap, that Paris.' I knew that would upset him. Turned redder than blood on a sacrificial altar. I won't have him saying anything against our Helen.

28

She's always been flighty — I don't mind saying it. But she is my sister and I won't have anyone else saying a word against her.

'Nice young chap!' he screeches. 'He was a guest. A GUEST!! He betrayed the trust of Menelaus. Nicked his wife while he was out hunting!'

'No need to shout,' I told him. 'You'll upset Iphigenia,' I said and patted our girl on the head.

'What's he on about, Mum?' Iphigenia asked.

'Your Auntie Helen's gone off to Troy with that nice Prince Paris,' I said.

'Oh, is that all?' she said and she went back to her sewing. Lovely girl our Iphigenia. Wish our other two, Orestes and Electra, were as good. Funny couple those two.

ORESTES AND ELECTRA

'Anyway,' Agamemnon says, 'There'll be trouble. Big trouble. They reckon we'll get a thousand ships and sail after her. Bring her back.'

'That'll take months!' I said.

'A Greek's got to do what a Greek's got to do,' he said. 'Now let me have a bit of supper, then I'll be off to organize the army.'

'Organize the army?' I said. 'Don't tell me you're going as well!'

'Going? Going? I'm leading the whole expedition. Menelaus is my brother, after all.'

That's Agamemnon all over. Getting into somebody else's fight. Just an excuse to go off and have a battle. Leaves me stuck here for months on end. It would serve him right if I did what Helen did and found myself a toy-boy. That would teach him. In fact I've had my eye on that Aegisthus for a while now...

AEGISTHUS

But no. Our Iphigenia would be upset. I'll just let Agamemnon get on with it. I hope he gets sea-sick

AUTUMN

I'll kill him! I will kill Agamemnon. You'll not believe what he's done. If I'd had a sword in my hand I'd have killed him there and then. But he's gone now. I'll just have to wait. If it takes six months or six years till he gets back, I'll have my revenge. I'll have his blood, I will.

I'll never forgive him. I know he had

problems. A thousand ships waiting to sail to Troy and they couldn't even get out of the harbour at Aulis. The wind kept blowing them back. Week after week.

Of course, I knew that they went to the Oracle to ask for advice. But I never did find out what the Oracle told them. Very quiet he was when he came back.

'Well? What's to do?" I asked.

'Oh, a sacrifice,' he muttered. 'Just a sacrifice and the gods will turn the wind around.'

'That's all right then. What is it? A sheep? A Deer?'

He muttered something and started to leave the room. 'What was that?' I said. 'I'm not going deaf. I swear he didn't _want_ me to hear.

'Er... a maiden. We have to sacrifice a maiden,' he said, ashamed like.

'Eeh, our Agamemnon. You're never going to kill a little girl just to get that useless trollop Helen back, are you?'

'A Greek's got to do....'

'Yeah, what a Greek's got to do. I know. I think it's a wicked shame. I just feel sorry for the lass's mother, that's all.'

'Aye,' he said, sheepish like, and slipped out.

I was so upset. I have to say, I was upset at the thought of them brutes slaughtering a young girl just to keep some god happy. So I sent for our little Iphigenia to cheer me up.

Her nurse was pale as a marble statue when I called her. 'Iphigenia's gone for the sacrifice,' she said.

'Gone to the sacrifice!' I cried. 'She's too young to go watching horrible things like that. She'll be upset. It'll put her off her dinner. She's a fussy eater at the best of times,' I said.

'No,' the nurse mumbled. 'She won't be having any dinner any more. Iphigenia's gone for the sacrifice. She is the sacrifice,' the poor woman explained.

I was speachless. That double-crossing filthy rat of a husband had our little girl killed on an altar just so he could go off and play soldiers.

Of course the winds turned and he set sail before I could get my hands on him. Left me here with the 'funny couple', Orestes and Electra, to bring up.

But I can wait. Oh, I can wait. The waiting'll just make it all the nicer when I finally get him. But, believe me, I'll get him. If he doesn't get killed at Troy he'll get killed when he gets ~~come~~ back home. I can wait.

FIVE YEARS LATER

Its not as easy taking Troy as they expected. Their little game of soldiers isn't as exciting as they thought. Sitting outside the walls of Troy every day. They must be bored out of their tiny minds.

I was bored myself. But now I've got that nice, sensible Aegisthus to keep me company — sensible enough not to go to Troy.

It'll serve Agamemnon right if he gets killed. But now I've got Aegisthus to help me its <u>certain</u> the old fool will be killed if he ever gets home. I've now got <u>two</u> reasons to get rid of him. I still haven't forgotten Iphigenia.

As for the 'funny couple', they're as strange as ever. Sometimes I think they don't love their Mother at all. That's fine, because I don't think much of them either.

ANOTHER FIVE YEARS LATER

So he's home. The conquering hero's home. Couldn't beat the Trojans in a fair fight so he beat them with a trick horse or something. Hid soldiers inside a wooden horse, they say.

WOODEN HORSE

Typical sneaky trick from Agamemnon. Poor Helen's back with Menelaus and everybody's happy... except me. And the Trojans of course

I pretended to welcome Agamemnon back like a loving wife, didn't I? But it was difficult when that girl stepped forward. 'This is Cassandra,' he said.

'Cassandra? Isn't she the King of Troy's daughter?'

'She is – and she is my wife-to-be.' he smirked.

'You've got a wife. You've got me!'

'Cassandra will be my second wife,' he said and marched into the palace. That scrawny girl trailed after him. They say she has the gift of prophecy. In that case she knows that we're going to kill her too. I could see it in her eyes. She knows. She knows

NEXT DAY

It's done. He's dead. We waited till he climbed into his bath. I walked in with the sword. I could have struck him from behind. But I wanted him to know what was going to happen — just as Iphigenia must have known ten years ago. Aegisthus finished him off. It was messy.

Cassandra was in her room. Waiting. As if she expected me. Perhaps she did. She didn't cry out or try to run away. She just closed her eyes and bowed her head.

It was harder than killing him in a way. Still, it's over now. Oh, yes, Electra and Orestes, the funny people, have had their heads together, hatching some kind of plot. They can't do anything. It's against every law of god or man to kill your own mother. I'm safe.

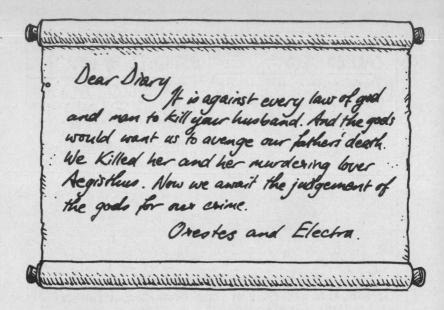

Dear Diary
        It is against every law of god
and man to kill your husband. And the gods
would want us to avenge our father's death.
We killed her and her murdering lover
Aegisthus. Now we await the judgement of
the gods for our crime.
                        Orestes and Electra.

The gods decided to destroy Orestes and Electra for killing their mother and sent the 'Furies' after them – sort of avenging angels. In the end the goddess, Athena, gave them a pardon.

That was the sort of story the Greeks liked to watch on the stage. People say that today's films and television programmes are too violent. But the truth is, entertainment has provided violent stories for thousands of years.

The truth about Troy
But was the story of Troy a 'history' story? Did it really happen? Homer was writing hundreds of years after the event. Of course, the story could have been passed down by word of mouth through the Dark Ages. Ask a historian . . .

WAS THERE A PLACE CALLED TROY?

YES. ARCHAEOLOGISTS HAVE FOUND THE SITE OF THE RUINS

• TROY

TURKEY

RUINS? SO WAS IT DESTROYED BY WAR?

IT WAS DESTROYED AND REBUILT SEVERAL TIMES ONCE IT WAS DESTROYED BY AN EARTHQUAKE

DID HELEN OF TROY REALLY EXIST?

DON'T KNOW. BUT IT WASN'T UNUSUAL FOR RAIDERS TO CARRY OFF QUEENS. SHE *COULD* HAVE EXISTED

AND WHAT ABOUT THE SACRIFICE OF IPHIGENIA?

POSSIBLE. THERE WERE CERTAINLY CASES OF CHILDREN BEING SACRIFICED – AND EVEN PARTLY EATEN – IN THOSE DAYS

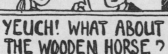

YEUCH! WHAT ABOUT THE WOODEN HORSE?

INTERESTING, THAT ONE. IT COULD HAVE BEEN A POETIC IDEA FOR A WOODEN BATTERING-RAM

... IT WOULD HAVE HAD A COVER TO KEEP THE DEFENDERS' ARROWS OFF THE ATTACKERS. THE COVER COULD HAVE BEEN HORSE-SHAPED

Don't tell tales

As well as plays, the ancient Greeks liked a good story. And nobody told better stories than Aesop. They are still popular today. Everybody's heard of *The Tortoise and the Hare*. The moral of that story is, 'Slow and steady wins the race'. Or *The Boy who Cried Wolf*, the moral of this story being, 'No one believes a liar – even if they start telling the truth.'

He gave us wise proverbs like, 'Never count your chickens before they're hatched'. But the most terrible tale of all is about Aesop himself.

Aesop was a Greek folk hero wno is supposed to have lived in the 6th century BC. One legend says he was born in Thrace, lived for a while as a slave on Sámos Island, was set free and travelled round the other states telling his stories.

Then he arrived at Delphi where the Oracle was. In ancient Greece, a priest or priestess who passed on advice from the gods was called an Oracle. Aesop seems to have upset the priests of the Oracle. Maybe he told the story of . . .

The man and the wooden god
In the old days, men used to worship sticks and stones and idols, and prayed to them to give them luck. It happened that a man had often prayed to a wooden idol he had received from his father, but his luck never seemed to change. He prayed and he prayed, but still he remained as unlucky as ever.

One day in the greatest rage he went to the wooden god, and with one blow swept it down from its stand. The idol broke in two, and what did he see? An immense number of coins flying all over the place.

And the moral of the story is, 'Religion is just a con trick created to make money for the priests.'

Whatever Aesop said, the priests didn't like it one little bit. They took him to the top of a cliff and threw him down to his death.

THE SAVAGE SPARTANS

The first great state to grow after the Dark Ages was Sparta. The Spartan people were a bit odd. They believed they were better than anyone else. If the Spartans wanted more land then they just moved into someone else's patch. If someone was already living there the Spartans just made them slaves. In short, they were the ungrooviest lot in the whole of Greece.

YOU HAVE A CHOICE, GIVE UP ALL YOUR LAND AND POSSESSIONS AND BECOME OUR SLAVE, OR WE KILL YOU

HMM... TRICKY ONE

Of course, a lot of people didn't enjoy being slaves. They argued with the Spartans in the only language the Spartans knew – the language of violence. They were probably the toughest of the Greek peoples because they were always having to fight to prove how good they were.

But it wasn't enough to train young men to fight. The training started from the day you were born.

Ten foul facts
1 Children were trained for fitness with running, wrestling, throwing quoits and javelins – and that was just the girls!
2 Girls also had to strip for processions, dances and temple services. That way they wouldn't learn to show off with fine clothes.

3 The marriage custom of Sparta was for a young man to pretend to carry his bride off by violence. The bride then cut off her hair and dressed like a man. The bridegroom rejoined the army and had to sneak off to visit his new wife.

4 A new-born baby was taken to be examined by the oldest Spartans. If it looked fit and strong they said, 'Let it live.' If it looked a bit sickly it was taken up a mountain and left to die.

5 A child didn't belong to its parents – it belonged to the State of Sparta. At the age of seven a child was sent off to join a 'herd' of children. The toughest child was allowed to become leader and order the others about. The old men who watched over them often set the children fighting amongst each other to see who was the toughest.

6 At the age of 12 they were allowed a cloak but no tunic. They were only allowed a bath a few times a year.

THAT THASOS IS A CLEANLINESS FREAK

YEAH...THAT'S HIS THIRD BATH THIS YEAR

7 Children slept on rushes that they gathered from the river bank themselves. If they were cold in winter then they mixed a few thistles in with the reeds . . . the prickling gave them a feeling of warmth.

8 The Spartan children were kept hungry. They were then encouraged to steal food – sneakiness is a good skill if you're out on a battlefield. If they were caught stealing they'd be beaten. They weren't beaten for stealing, you understand – they were beaten for being careless enough to get caught. Sometimes the young men were beaten just to toughen them up. If the beating killed the youth then it was just bad luck.

YOU SHOULD BE A LOT TOUGHER NOW... DEAD, BUT TOUGHER

9 Older boys had younger boys to serve them. If the younger boy did something wrong then a common punishment was a bite on the back of the hand.

10 If you cried out while you were fighting then not only were you punished but your best friend was punished as well.

Of course, the savage Spartans were no worse than some of their enemies, such as the Scythians. The historian, Herodotus (485 – 425 BC), described the horrors of the Scythians . . .

> *In a war, it is the custom of a Scythian soldier to drink the blood of the first man he kills. The heads of all enemies killed in battle are taken to the king; a head represents a token which allows the soldier a share in the loot – no head no loot. He strips the skin off the head by*

> *making a circular cut round the ears and shaking out the skull; then he scrapes the flesh off the skin with an ox's rib, and when it is clean works it supple with his fingers. He hangs these trophies on the bridle of his horse like handkerchiefs and is very proud of them. The finest warrior is the one who has the most scalps. Many Scythians sew scalps together to make cloaks and wear them like the cloak of a peasant.*

The boy who didn't cry 'fox'

One Spartan story shows you how peculiar the Spartans really were. It's a story about a good little Spartan boy.

How to be a good Spartan 1: Pinch whatever you like – but don't get caught

He stole a fox cub belonging to somebody else.

How to be a good Spartan 2: Don't give up without a struggle

The boy was seen running away from the scene of the theft and arrested. But before they caught him he just had time to stuff the fox cub up his tunic.

How to be a good Spartan 3: Cheat, lie and trick your way out of trouble

The boy's master asked the boy where the fox cub was. The boy replied, 'Fox cub? What fox cub? I don't know anything about a fox cub!'

How to be a good Spartan 4: It's better to be a dead hero than a live whinger

The master's questioning went on . . . and on. Until suddenly the boy fell down. Dead. When the guards examined the body they found the fox cub had eaten its way into the boy's guts. The tough Spartan lad hadn't given any sign that he was suffering and he hadn't given in, even though it cost him his life.

Could you be as boldly deceitful as the Spartan boy?

LOOKS LIKE HE CHOKED ON HIS UNFINISHED MATHS HOMEWORK

Thermopylae

The story of the boy and the fox might not be true – it simply shows the sort of people the Spartans admired. But the story of the battle of Thermopylae is almost certainly true. Again it shows the Spartans dying rather than giving in.

There were just 300 Spartans led by King Leonidas defending the narrow pass of Thermopylae against tens of thousands of Persians. The Persian leader, Xerxes, sent spies to report how many soldiers were defending the pass. He couldn't believe the Spartans would be daft enough to fight and die. Xerxes didn't know the Spartans.

But the Spartans were not just unafraid. They were really cool about it. They spent the time before the battle oiling their bodies and combing their hair – now that *was* groovy.

How to be a good Spartan 5: When you're in trouble, think of something witty to say
The Spartans were warned that the Persians had so many archers that their arrows would blot out the sun. Dioneces, the Spartan general, said, 'That's good. We'll have a bit of shade to fight the battle.'

How to be a good Spartan 6: Stay cooler than an iced lolly
The Spartans held on for a week. Then a traitor guided the Persians to a secret pathway that led them behind the Spartans. The 300 Spartans were massacred. As they fought to the death some lost their swords. They battled on with their fists and their teeth.

Could you stay as cool as a Spartan in danger?

Did you know . . . ?
One horrible historical way of proving you were a good Spartan was to be whipped at the altar of the god, Artemis. The one who suffered the most lashes was the toughest. Bleeding half to death – sometimes *all the way* to death – but *tough*. Ah yes, a *perfect* Spartan.

The spooky Spartan
Pausanius was a great Spartan general who helped to defeat the Persians in 479 BC. But the Spartans thought he was getting too big-headed and they asked him to return to Sparta to explain – or be punished.

Pausanius was not amused. He wrote to the Persian king, Xerxes, and offered to betray Sparta. Off went the messenger to Xerxes. But that messenger wondered why other messengers before him hadn't come back. So he opened the letter and read it. There on the end was a little message for Xerxes . . .

The messenger took the letter to the Spartans instead of to Xerxes – wouldn't you? The Spartans sent a force to kill Pausanius. The general fled to the temple of Athena where he sheltered in a small building. 'You can't lay a finger on me here. I'm on sacred ground,' he said.

'Right,' the leader of the assassins said. 'We won't lay a finger on you.' And they didn't. They just bricked up the door and left him to starve to death. That should have been the end of Pausanius. The trouble was his ghost started wandering round the temple making such hideous noises that the priestess was losing customers. In the end she sent for a magician – a sort of groovy Greek Ghostbuster – to get rid of him . . . finally.

THE ODD ATHENIANS

Deadly Draco

The people of Athens were very different from the Spartans. One of their first rulers was a man called Draco. The Athenians thought the Spartans were pretty brutal, but the laws of Draco were nearly as cruel. He wrote the first law book for Athens, and criminals were executed for almost any crime. Under Draco's laws . . .

● you could have someone made your personal slave if they owed you money

● the theft of an apple or a cabbage was punishable by death

● people found guilty of idleness would be executed.

> I WASN'T IDLE. I WAS ASLEEP!

Draco said . . .

> *Yes, it's unfair. Little crimes and big crimes get the same punishment. If only I could think of a punishment worse than death for the serious ones.*

Seven hundred years later a Greek writer, Plutarch, said . . .

> *Draco's laws were not written in ink but in blood.*

Other Greeks thought that Draco's laws were better than no laws. (The people who thought this were not the ones who Draco had executed, of course.)

Playful Peisistratus

Another ruler, Peisistratus, wasn't so quite so harsh. He was still a 'tyrant' – in Greece that was someone who took control of the state by force – but he stayed there only as long as the people agreed with what he was doing.

Peisistratus made the people pay heavy taxes – ten per cent of all they earned – but at least he had a sense of humour.

One day he visited a farmer. The farmer didn't recognize Peisistratus.

'WHAT DO YOU GET OUT OF THIS LAND?'

'NOTHING BUT ACHES AND PAINS, I WISH PEISISTRATUS WOULD TAKE HIS TEN PER CENT OF THOSE'

Peisistratus laughed – and ordered that the old farmer need never pay taxes again.

Plotting Peisistratus

Peisistratus became very unpopular and the people of Athens were turning against him. Then one day he drove his cart into the market place in a terrible state. He and his mules were cut and bleeding. 'I've been attacked by assassins!' he cried. 'I barely escaped with my life.'

HOW COME HE GETS ALL THE ATTENTION?

The Athenians were worried they would lose their leader – not a popular leader, but the only leader they had. They organized the strongest and most brutal Athenian men to be his bodyguards. He then used them to seize control of the city.

The attack on Peisistratus had put him in power. Just as he meant it to. For there had been *no* attack. The crafty leader had simply made the wounds himself!

Who killed the ox?

The Athenians weren't as ruthless as the Spartans. But they had their own funny little ways. One of the strangest customs of Athens involved the sacrifice of an ox in the temple. Killing the ox wasn't strange in itself. It's what the Athenians did *afterwards* that was curious. They held a trial to decide, 'Who killed the ox?'

Horrible hemlock

The Athenians didn't just have strange ways of killing knives. They also killed each other in unusual ways.

After they had lost the war with Sparta the Athenians looked for someone to blame. They blamed the old teacher, Socrates. Being a rather groovy guy, he was always hanging around with young people, telling them not to believe in the old gods. (That's a bit like your own teacher telling you not to believe in Father Christmas.) In Athens this was punishable by death.

But the Athenians didn't kill the old teacher – they told him to kill himself with poison! Plato described the gruesome scene . . .

> *The man who was to give the poison came in with it ready mixed in a cup. Socrates saw him and said, 'Good Sir, you understand these things. What do I have to do?'*
>
> *'Just drink it and walk around until your legs begin to feel heavy, then lie down. It works very quickly.'*
>
> *The man gave Socrates the cup.*
>
> *The teacher took it cheerfully, without trembling, and without even turning pale. He just looked at the man and said, 'May I drink a toast?'*
>
> *'You may,' the man replied.*
>
> *'Then I drink to the gods and pray that we will be just as happy after death as we were in life.'*

Then he drank the poison quickly and cheerfully. Until then most of us had held back our tears. But when we saw him drinking, the tears came in floods. I covered my face and wept – not for him but for myself, I had lost such a good friend.

Socrates looked at us and said sternly, 'I have heard that a person should be allowed to die in silence. So control yourselves and be quiet.' We stopped crying.

The teacher lay down. The man with the poison squeezed his foot. Socrates said he felt nothing. He said that when the poison reached the heart he would be gone.

As the numbness reached his waist Socrates called to young Crito. He said, 'Crito, we owe Asclepius a sacrifice. Be sure you pay him. Don't forget.'

[Asclepius was the god of healing.]

'Of course,' Crito replied. 'Is there anything else you want?'

But Socrates didn't reply.

This was the end of our friend. The best, wisest and most honest person I have ever known.

What a hero! Probably the only teacher in history to die so nobly. Would your teacher be as brave?

Unfortunately you'll never have the chance to find out . . . Boots the Chemist does not sell hemlock.

Dreadful democracy

Most countries today are run as *democracies* – that is to say every adult has a vote on which laws are passed and how the government spends its money.

Athens, being really groovy, had the *first* democracy. But because they still had a lot to learn, they didn't quite get it right . . .

THE POWER OF THE PERSIANS

King Darius of Persia had a large army and decided it was about time he took over Greece as well. He didn't bother going to the battle personally – he thought the Greeks would be a pushover. They *should* have been a pushover because . . .

● there was only the Athenian army to stop them – the Spartans were too busy at a religious festival and they missed the battle

● the Greek soldiers were a bit frightened by the appearance of the Persian soldiers.

The Persians were wearing trousers while the Greeks wore groovy *skirts*.

Still, the Athenian Greeks won the great battle at a place called Marathon.

That kept the Persians away for about ten years.

Then along came the new Persian king, Xerxes, with an absolutely *huge* army.

There were too many soldiers to transport across the Hellespont – a stretch of water almost 1200 metres wide between Greece and Persia – so Xerxes built a bridge.

A storm came and smashed the bridge. Xerxes was cross – yes, I know there are *two* crosses in Xerxes, but I don't mean that sort of cross. He was furious.

#!!*✲!

MORE LIKE *BERSERXES* IF YOU ASK ME

So, what did the potty Persian do?

1 Ordered the bridge builder to be given three hundred lashes.

2 Ordered the sea at Hellespont to receive three hundred lashes.

3 Ordered the army to swim across.

Answer: 2 Xerxes ordered that the sea should receive the lashes and have iron shackles thrown in as a punishment. One story even said he sent torturers to brand the sea with burning irons.

Paper-headed Persians
The Greeks wouldn't have feared the Persians so much if they'd known what the great historian Herodotus knew. He told a remarkable story about an earlier Persian battlefield – at Pelusium in Egypt where the Persians had fought in 525 BC.

On the battlefield I saw a strange thing which the natives pointed out to me. The bones of the dead lay scattered on the field in two lots – those of the Persians and those of the Egyptians. If, then, you strike a Persian skull (even with a pebble) they are so weak you will break a hole in them. But the Egyptian skulls are so strong that you may hit them with a rock and hardly crack them.

The wooden wall

After slaughtering the Spartans, Xerxes headed south towards Athens. The Athenians retreated to the island of Salamis, just off the coast of Athens. They had to watch while Xerxes burned Athens to the ground.

But the Athenian leader was a groovy Greek called Themistocles. He went to the temple at Delphi and asked for advice from the 'Oracle' – a kind of adviser on behalf of the gods. The Oracle told him to 'put his trust in the wooden wall'. What did he do?

1 Build a navy (of wooden ships).
2 Build a wooden fence around the island of Salamis to keep the Persians out.
3 Build a wooden fence around Athens to keep the Persians in.

The spooky ship of Salamis

Herodotus also reported a strange happening at the battle of Salamis . . .

The Athenians tell this story about a captain from Corinth called Adeimantus. As the battle started he was filled with fear and dread; he hoisted his sails and hurried from the fight. When the other Corinthians saw this they turned to follow him. But just as they reached the temple of Athena on Salamis, a ship came alongside them. It was a ship of the gods for no man sent it. A voice from the strange ship called, 'Would you betray your Greek friends, Adeimantus? They are now winning the battle. Turn back and help.' The Corinthian said it was a lie. The voice replied, 'You can take this ship and destroy it if you find out I am lying. Turn back, turn back.' So Adeimantus and the Corinthians joined the battle again and helped the Greeks to win. But no one was able to tell him where the strange ship had come from . . .

58

Maybe it was a 'ghost ship'. Another story says the Corinthians only *pretended* to run away. It was all part of a cunning Athenian plan. The Corinthians' trick led the Persians into a trap. They then turned and attacked them when they least expected it. There never was a ship of the gods.

Which story do you believe? One fact is that lots of sailors died. Two horrible historical epitaphs read . . .

> HE WENT DOWN WITH HIS SHIP AND WHERE HIS BONES ARE ROTTING ONLY THE SEABIRD KNOWS

And . . .

> SAILORS, DON'T ASK WHOSE BODY LIES HERE. I WISH YOU BETTER LUCK THAN MINE AND A KINDER SEA

Peloponnesian wars

Xerxes the Persian went home after he lost the sea battle at Salamis. His son-in-law, Mardonius, wanted to stay and batter a few more Greeks, so Xerxes left him to get on with it. Mardonius was killed and his army defeated.

Of course, the Athenians were really pleased with themselves. They decided to get all the Greek states to team up in case the Persians ever came back. The trouble was the Athenians wanted to be the captain of the team.

Sparta weren't having that. They decided not to play. After that it was just a matter of time before Athens and Sparta fought each other to see who was best. And that was the start of the Peloponnesian War.

Awful armies

Alcibiades was a great Athenian general – but a terrible poser. He dressed in the grooviest clothes and would do anything to draw attention to himself. Once he cut off the tail of his favourite dog so that people would take notice.

I WONDER IF THEY'D NOTICE HIM MORE IF I BIT HIS NOSE OFF?

Half of Athens (especially the women) loved him – but the men in power hated him and wanted him dead. They sent him off to fight the Spartans while they plotted against him.

Alcibiades led the Athenian army in the attack on the Spartan allies at Syracuse (in Sicily) between 415 and 413 BC. But he was called back to Athens because he was charged with 'sacrilege' – that's being nasty to the gods. He was supposed to have gone to some statues of gods and knocked off their noses – and (because the statues didn't have any clothes on) he knocked off their 'naughty bits' as well.

Of course, clever Alcibiades knew they'd probably kill him for this. So he *didn't* go back to Athens, sensible man. He went over to the enemy – *Sparta*. He told the Spartans all the secrets of the Athenian army. The Spartans went and helped Syracuse.

THE PELOPONNESIAN WAR LEAGUE RESULTS

SPARTA & SYRACUSE UNITED 1 – ATHENS 0

Of course, Alcibiades came to a sticky end – just like the tail of his dog, really! The Spartans had him assassinated rather than let him switch back to fighting for Athens.

A group of men arrived at his house to kill him but hadn't the nerve to fight him face to face – even though they outnumbered him. First they set his house on fire. When Alcibiades came out into the open, carrying his sword, they shot him full of arrows from a safe distance.

Wonderful weapons

During the Peloponnesian wars, Greeks were fighting Greeks. If you know how your enemy fights, you can stop him – and at the same time he can stop you. Every battle becomes a 0–0 draw. What you need are some secret weapons to surprise and frighten the enemy.

That's what the groovy Greek army from Boetia came up with. Here's what they made . . .

61

TOP SECRET

THE BOETIAN BLASTER

1 CUT DOWN A TALL STRAIGHT TREE, TRIM THE BRANCHES OFF THEN SPLIT THE TRUNK IN TWO

2 HOLLOW OUT THE TRUNK THEN JOIN THE TWO HALVES TOGETHER, YOU NOW HAVE A HOLLOW TUBE LIKE A FLUTE

3 HANG A METAL VESSEL FULL OF SMOULDERING COALS, TAR AND SULPHUR AT ONE END AND A BELLOWS AT THE OTHER END

4 CARRY THE MACHINE TO A PLACE WHERE THE ENEMY WALLS ARE MOSTLY MADE OF WOOD. AIM THE TUBE AT THE WALLS AND SQUEEZE THE BELLOWS.

PROTECTION FROM ENEMY ARROWS

5 A HUGE FLAME WILL SHOOT OUT OF THE METAL VESSEL, SETTING FIRE TO THE WALLS AND DRIVING THE DEFENDERS AWAY

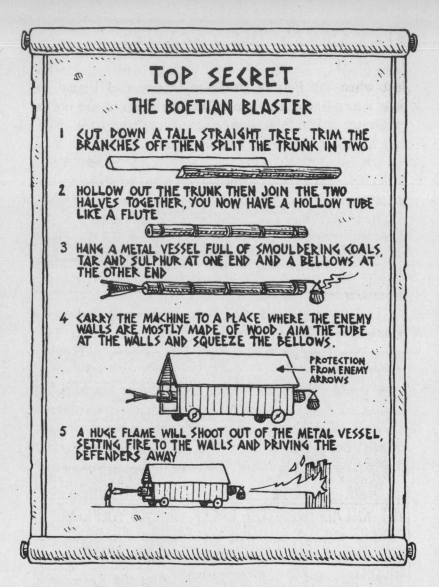

It worked! The Boetians captured the city of Delium with it. They had invented the world's first *flame thrower!*

ALEXANDER THE GREAT-ER

Just when the Persian threat to Greece had begun to fade, a new one came from a small kingdom in the north of Greece called Macedon. Some historians have even said that Macedon wasn't Greek at all.

First came Philip, king of Macedon. He defeated the Athenians and then told them he wanted them to attack the old enemy . . . Persia.

Then there was a small hitch in Philip's plan . . . he died. But that was only a tiny complication for the plan. (A rather bigger complication for Philip, of course.) Philip's son was greater and even groovier than him. Alexander the Great-er in fact . . .

Alexander - This is Your Life

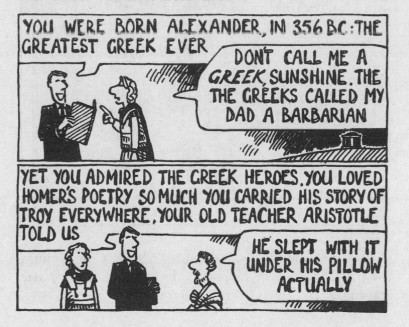

The knotty problem

Alexander entered Gordium and was told that the wagon of King Gordius was tied to its shafts with a knot that no one could untie. A legend said that the man who finally untied it would rule all Asia. How did Alexander unfasten the wagon from its shafts?

Answer: He took out his sword and cut through the knot.

THINK LIKE A GREEK

The Greeks were very superstitious people. They believed in horoscopes and ghosts and the gods deciding your fate. They believed that the gods spoke through 'Oracles' and you could learn about the future . . . if you understood the Oracle.

Awesome Oracles

The Greeks liked to know what would happen in the future. They didn't have crystal balls or people reading your palm. Instead they had Oracles. You went to a holy place, made a sacrifice and asked a god to tell you what the future held.

Of course, the god didn't speak to a human directly. There were a couple of ways of getting your message. At Delphi, the god Apollo spoke through his Oracle priestess. She was a bit like a medium in a seance today. She went into a trance and spoke in a strange language. The priests then took this baffling information and told the visitor what it meant.

The priests at Delphi actually could give good advice. So many visitors came, with so much gossip, that the priests of Delphi knew more than most people about what was going on in the Greek states.

Croesus the crafty

There were several Oracles in Greece. Crafty King Croesus decided to test them to see which was the most accurate.

He sent seven messengers to seven Oracles. They all had to ask the same question at the same time . . . *What is King Croesus doing at this very moment?*

They brought their replies back to the king. The Oracle of Delphi's answer was a curious one. It said ...

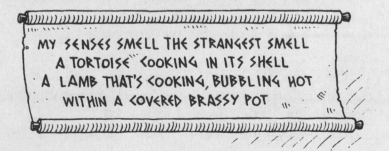

MY SENSES SMELL THE STRANGEST SMELL
A TORTOISE COOKING IN ITS SHELL
A LAMB THAT'S COOKING, BUBBLING HOT
WITHIN A COVERED BRASSY POT

Croesus was impressed. He'd deliberately chosen the daftest thing he could think of to do on that day. So he cut up a tortoise and a lamb and made a stew of them. He cooked them in a brass cauldron with a lid.

Croesus decided the Oracle of Delphi was the one to believe. Crafty Croesus. But. . .

Double-crossed Croesus

But the priests also cheated a bit. They gave curious answers that could mean more than one thing. King Croesus of Lydia spoke to the Oracle when he was about to go to war with Persia.

'What will happen if I attack Persia?' King Croesus asked.

'In the battle a great empire will be destroyed,' the Oracle said.

Croesus went off happily into battle – and lost! Lydia was destroyed. He thought the Oracle meant that *Persia* would be destroyed.

Some of the Greeks' favourite stories were about the Oracle. Many were about the ancient game of . . .

Beat the Oracle

The Bacchiad family ruled Corinth. They were rich and powerful . . . and they were worried. Big Bacchiad had just come back from the Oracle with a threatening message.

'The Oracle has said, "Labda will give birth to a rock that will roll down on those who rule and he will put all Corinth right,"' Big Bacchiad told them.

'Put all Corinth right?' Mrs Bacchiad sniffed.

'Nothing wrong with Corinth. . . at least, not while we're in charge.'

'That's not the point,' Little Bacchiad pointed out. 'If the gods say it's curtains for us, then it's curtains for us.'

'Hah! Just like a man, talking like that. Listen, if the Oracle says she's giving birth to the child who'll defeat us, we simply kill the child.'

'That's murder that is,' Big Bacchiad frowned. 'We'd never get away with it.'

'Not if the baby has an *accident*,' Mrs Bacchiad grinned an evil grin.

'Not much chance of that,' Little Bacchiad sighed.

'Oh, but there is if we *make* it have an accident,' the woman explained. 'As soon as the baby is born, we go visiting. Ask to see the new baby.'

'That's nice,' Big Bacchiad said.

'No it's not,' Mrs Bacchiad said with a slow shake of the head. 'Whoever she hands the baby to will drop it.'

'Drop it!' Little Bacchiad squeaked.

'On the stone floor,' the woman said grimly. 'On its head. End of problem.'

69

Of course it wasn't that simple. With the Oracle it never is. The baby was born and the Bacchiads went to visit. Mrs Bacchiad left the house ten minutes later. Her face was white with bright red spots of anger on her chubby cheeks.

'I cannot believe it. All you had to do was drop the baby. *Drop the baby!* That's what we agreed. Why did you not drop it?'

Big Bacchaid gave a faint and sheepish smile. 'It smiled at me. I couldn't drop the little feller while he was smiling at me, could I? I hadn't the heart.'

'Heart? It's not heart you're short of – it's brain,' the woman seethed. She turned to Little Bacchiad. 'Tonight you go back with a club. You creep into the house and you kill the child. Understand?'

Little Bacchiad nodded. 'I won't let you down,' he promised.

But Labda had seen Mrs Bacchiad's face when the man handed the baby back to her. She knew the woman wanted the baby dead. So that night she hid the child in a wooden chest. It slept safely and woke the next day still smiling.

70

Labda called the baby Cypselus – after the word meaning chest. Cypselus grew up a popular and groovy leader, while the Bacchiad family were hated in Corinth. The young man became king of Corinth – a strong king but a good-natured one. However, when it came to the Bacchiads he was quite, quite ruthless.

Cypselus was the rock that would roll down on those who ruled . . . and, like a rock, he crushed them. Just as the Oracle predicted.

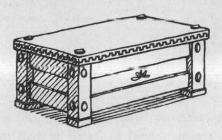

Did you know . . . ?
The Pythian Oracle at Delphi inhaled smoke from the burning leaves of certain trees to help them see into the future. The leaves gave off a drug that put them into a trance.

But at the Corinth Oracle there were cheats at work. There you could actually speak directly to a god! You spoke to the altar . . . and a voice boomed back from beneath your feet with the answer.

Was it a miracle? The visitors believed it was. But today's archaeologists know better. They found a secret tunnel that led under the altar. A priest could crawl along and lie under the feet of the visitor. He could listen to the questions and speak an answer through a funnel into a tube.

Greek superstitions

The Greeks had some of the cleverest thinkers of ancient times. Yet, in some ways, they had some very strange beliefs.

People today are nervous about walking under a ladder because they think it will bring them bad luck, or they touch wood to bring them good luck. The Greeks had their own strange superstitions. They believed. . .

1 Birds were messengers between earth and heaven, and the moon was a resting place for spirits on their way to heaven.

2 The Greeks believed that Hecate was the goddess of witchcraft and crossroads. She would appear at crossroads on clear nights, along with ghosts and howling phantom dogs. The Greeks left food at crossroads for her. (She was also asked for help with curing madness – the Greeks believed madness was caused by the spirits of the dead.)

3 The Greeks looked at the guts of dead birds and believed they could read the future from them.

4 They also thought there were spirits called 'daimons' around. Some were good and protected you; some were evil and could lead you into wickedness. Even clever people like Socrates believed in daimons. His own daimon warned him of trouble ahead . . . and it never let him down.

5 Sometimes the Greeks kept dead bodies in jars called *pithos*. But sometimes, they said, the spirits of the dead escaped from the jars and began to bother the living with illness and disease. These wicked spirits were called *keres*. The best way to stop the keres from getting into your house was to paint tar round your door frames. That way the keres would stick to the tar and not be able to get into the house.

WHAT DO THEY SAY?

IN THE FUTURE THERE WILL BE FEWER BIRDS

IT WASN'T ME SIR, IT WAS MY DAIMON

6 The Greeks believed that if you dreamed about seeing your reflection in a mirror then you would die soon after. But don't worry, because you would soon be born again. According to some Greeks you are in three parts . . .

- body
- soul
- mind

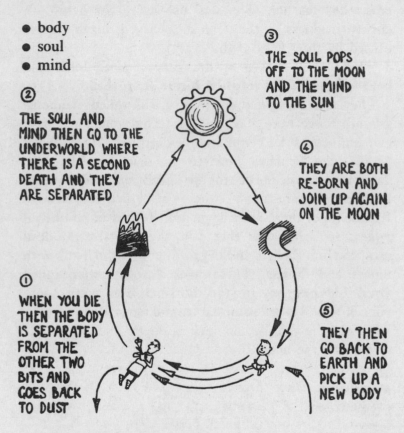

② THE SOUL AND MIND THEN GO TO THE UNDERWORLD WHERE THERE IS A SECOND DEATH AND THEY ARE SEPARATED

③ THE SOUL POPS OFF TO THE MOON AND THE MIND TO THE SUN

④ THEY ARE BOTH RE-BORN AND JOIN UP AGAIN ON THE MOON

① WHEN YOU DIE THEN THE BODY IS SEPARATED FROM THE OTHER TWO BITS AND GOES BACK TO DUST

⑤ THEY THEN GO BACK TO EARTH AND PICK UP A NEW BODY

7 They also believed that the left side is bad – the right side is good. Many people still believe that today – they try to force left-handed children to write with their right hand, for example.

74

Potty Pythagoras

The famous teacher, Pythagoras, set up his own religion. The Pythagoreans believed that the soul lived on after death and went into another body. One day Pythagoras saw a man beating a dog and heard it yelping. He told the man . . .

'STOP! STOP! THAT'S MY DEAR FRIEND. I RECOGNISE HIS VOICE!'

In fact it wasn't safe to have anything to do with butchers or huntsmen – when they killed that cow or that deer they may have murdered your dead mother.

They also thought that if they behaved themselves they might come back as a great person. If they were naughty in this life they'd come back as something nasty – a pig, a dog, even a tree. And if you were really, really wicked you'd come back as the worst thing of all . . . a woman!

The Pythagoreans lived apart from the rest of the Greek people and had some rather strange rules. Does your teacher have strange rules? Then ask them which of these rules Pythagoras truly had. . . and which are false.

True or False
1 Don't eat beans.
2 Don't walk along the main street.
3 Don't touch the fire with an iron poker.

4 Don't touch a white cockerel.
5 Don't eat the heart of an animal.
6 Don't stand on your fingernail clippings.
7 Don't leave the mark of your body on a bed when you get up.
8 Don't look in a mirror beside a lamp.
9 Help a man to load something – but don't help anyone to unload.
10 Don't pick your nose with the fingers of your left hand.

Answer: 10 is false. All the rest are true. Some Greeks believed that beans contained the souls of the dead and would never eat them.

The ghostly Greeks
The groovy Greeks told the first ghost stories. But it was a Roman, Pliny, who first wrote this one down.

Dear Lucias

I have just heard this strange story which I think might interest you.

In Athens there used to be a large and beautiful house which was supposed to be badly haunted. Locals told how horrid noises were heard at the dead of night: the clanking of chains which grew louder and louder. Until there suddenly appeared the hideous phantom of an old man who was a picture of filth and misery. His beard was long and matted, his white hair wild and uncombed. His thin legs were loaded with a weight of chains that he dragged wearily along with a painful moaning; his wrists were fastened by long cruel links; while all the time he raised his arms and shook his shackles in a kind of helpless fury.

Some brave people were once bold enough to watch all night in the house. They were almost scared out of their senses at the sight of the spook. Even worse, disease and even death followed those who had braved a night in that house. The place was shunned. A 'For Sale' sign was put up but no one bought it and the house fell almost to ruin and decay.

But Athenodorus was poor. He rented it even though he knew the story of the ghost. On his first night there he sat working. He heard the rattling chain and saw the gruesome old man. The ghost beckoned him with a finger. Athenodorus said he was too busy. The ghost grew angry and rattled his chains still more. The young man stood up and followed the spook.

When they reached the garden the spirit pointed to a spot in the garden – then vanished. Athenodorus marked the spot, went to bed and had a peaceful night's sleep.

Next day he went to the law officers and told them what he had seen. They dug at the spot the young man had marked and found a skeleton... bound in chains.

When the body had been given a proper burial, peace returned to the house at night.

Pliny

77

Think like a Greek

In the summer of 413 BC the army of Athens was in trouble. They were trying to beat the town of Syracuse with a siege. But one of their leaders had been killed and the other leader, Nicias, was poorly with a fever.

The Athenians decided to pack up and go home. Everyone agreed this was a good idea and they began packing to go. But that night there was an eclipse of the full moon. The soldiers said this was a sign from the gods.

A sign of disaster, some said. A sign that they should stay . . . or a sign that they should go? They couldn't agree. They asked their leader, Nicias.

'We will forget any plan to return home. We must wait for the next full moon,' Nicias said.

He waited 27 more days. What happened?

1 Nicias died and the army went home.

2 They suffered disaster anyway.

3 The Syracuse army surrendered.

Answer: 2 The extra 27 days gave the Syracuse navy time to block off the river with rows of ships chained together. The Athenian ships couldn't get out of the river to get their army back home. Their army had to march across the land instead. The enemy were waiting and the Athenian army was wiped out. The ones who weren't killed were made into slaves. This disaster was the end of Athens as a great state . . . and all because of an eclipse of the moon and the superstitious nature of a Greek general.

LIVE LIKE A GREEK

Polybius' Checkerboard

The Greeks were also very groovy with numbers. Polybius, born in 200 BC, was a Greek historian of Rome. He was one of 1,000 hostages taken to Rome in 168 BC. His main history books contained 40 volumes, but he also had time to invent this code, now known as Polybius' Checkerboard.

Each letter has a pair of numbers – the horizontal (across) number followed by the vertical (up-down). So, 'B' is 1-2, but F is 2-1. The word 'Yes' is 54 15 43. Get it?

	1	2	3	4	5
1	A	B	C	D	E
2	F	G	H	I/J	K
3	L	M	N	O	P
4	Q	R	S	T	U
5	V	W	X	Y	Z

Then work out this . . .

44 23 15   22 23 15 15 25   44 15 11 13 23 15 42   11 33
11 53 24 32 11 33 14 15 42   12 42 34 45 22 23 44   44
23 15   21 24 42 43 44   43 45 33 - 14 24 11 31   44 34
22 42 15 15 13 15.

79

Did you know . . . ?

Polybius' Checkerboard may have been a good way of sending secret messages. But a Greek called Histiaeus found a better one!

He was imprisoned by the Persians but was allowed to send a letter to his cousin Aristagoras. The Persians studied the message carefully. They could see no code or secret meaning. The message was a perfectly harmless letter. They let a slave take the letter to Aristagoras.

As soon as the slave arrived he said to Aristagoras, 'Shave my head.' Aristagoras shaved the slave's head. Tattooed on his scalp was the real message. 'Lead a rebellion against the Persians.' Cool, eh?

Make a pinhole camera

The Greeks also invented other groovy devices which are still important to us today. One of the cleverest was the camera obscura – or the 'pinhole' camera. A Greek artist covered a window with a dark material, then punched a small hole through. An upside-down image of the scene was seen on the inside wall and traced by the artist.

You could have a go at making your own, slightly smaller version:

1 Make a box of black card, 20 x 10 x 10 cm.
2 Make a small pinhole in black paper at one end.
3 Place grease-proof paper across the other end.
4 Hold it up to a bright scene.
5 The scene will be 'projected' on to the grease-proof paper.

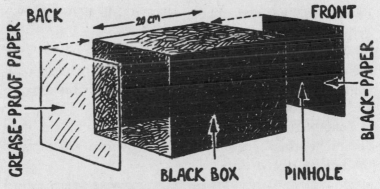

Note: this image will be upside-down – you may have to stand on your head to get the best view!

Making a dodgy drachma

The Greeks had banks. There are no records of bank robbers . . . but there were people who tried to cheat the banks out of lots of money. Here's how to do it. . .

1 Go to the bank and say, 'I want 10,000 drachmas to buy a ship. I'll fill it with corn and sell it on the other side of the Mediterranean. When the ship returns with the money for the corn I'll pay back the loan.'
2 The bank agrees. The Greek banks even agree that if the ship sinks (and you lose all their money) then you don't have to pay them a thing.
3 You buy a cheap ship and put a little bit of cheap corn in it. You spend about 5,000 drachmas and keep the other 5,000 drachmas for yourself.
4 Just as the ship reaches deep water you saw through the keel at the bottom of the boat. This will make it sink.
5 When the boat begins to sink you jump in the lifeboat, paddle back home and say to the bank, 'Sorry, you've lost your 10,000 drachmas!' and have a good laugh because you've earned yourself a quick 5,000 just for getting your feet wet.

Good idea, eh? And it nearly worked for the villainous ship owner, Hegestratos, and his partner, Zenothemis. But it all went wrong at stage 4.

Zenothemis kept the passengers chatting on the deck one night while Hegestratos crept down to saw through the bottom of the ship.

One of the passengers heard the noise and went down to investigate. Hegestratos was caught and had to escape. He fled along the deck and jumped into the waiting lifeboat. Or rather he *tried* to jump into the lifeboat. It was dark. He missed the little boat, fell in the sea . . . and drowned. Served him right.

The ship reached the shore safely and the bank got Zenothemis to pay back the money. So Hegestratos ended up dead . . . not rich.

Let the punishment fit the crime

Alexandria was a city in Egypt but ruled by the Greeks. Around 250 BC they had a set of laws which might give some idea of how the Greek law worked.

Can you match the crime to the punishment? Just remember the law wasn't completely fair. Especially if you were a slave.

Crime	Punishment
1 A free man strikes another free man or free woman.	a) A hundred lashes
2 A slave strikes a free man or free woman.	b) Fine of 100 drachmas
3 A drunk person injures somebody else.	c) A hundred lashes
4 A free man threatens another with wood, iron or bronze.	d) Fine of 100 drachmas
5 A slave threatens another with wood, iron or bronze.	e) Fine of 200 drachmas

83

If a master didn't want his slave to receive the 100 lashes then he had to pay 200 drachma, or 2 drachma a blow.

If you argued with a fine then you could go to court. But be careful. If you lost then you had to pay double for crime 1 or treble for crime 4.

Woe for women

Being a slave in ancient Greece wasn't much fun. Being a woman wasn't too groovy either. The Spartan women lived like men – the Athenian women lived like slaves. They were told what to do and what not to do – and they didn't have anything like the freedom that the free men enjoyed . . .

84

GREEK GOOD WIFE GUIDE

A WOMAN SHOULD	A WOMAN DOES NOT
• STAY AT HOME • BE BROUGHT UP WITH SLAVES AND LEARN HOUSEHOLD SKILLS • LEARN TO SPIN, WEAVE, COOK AND MANAGE SLAVES • HAVE A HUSBAND CHOSEN BY HER FATHER - WHEN SHE IS 15 • WORSHIP THE GODDESS HESTIA	• VOTE • BUY OR SELL ANYTHING WORTH MORE THAN A SMALL MEASURE OF BARLEY • OWN ANYTHING OTHER THAN HER CLOTHES, JEWELLERY AND SLAVES • LEAVE THE HOUSE EXCEPT TO VISIT OTHER WOMEN OR GO TO RELIGIOUS FESTIVALS AND FUNERALS

Groovy girls

The women of Attica, the region surrounding Athens, were different from the women living in Athens. They helped their husbands in the fields. They also had a curious way of preparing their daughters for marriage.

Girls aged about 13 were sent to the Brauron temple of the goddess, Artemis. There they prepared to be mature young women, and good wives, by doing what?

1 Learning how to fire bows and arrows, to throw spears, to mend armour and sharpen swords.

2 Praying to the goddess for wisdom, and learning the secret spells to keep husbands happy and healthy.

3 Running and dancing through the woods with no clothes on pretending to be she-bears.

Answer: 3 The idea was they got their wildness 'out of their systems' before they settled down to marriage. The Brauron temple proved very popular with Greek girls around 370 - 380 BC.

However, girls, you should *not* try this at your local place of worship – you'd only get arrested, or photographed by the boys in your class, or catch pneumonia . . . or all three.

I'M BEGINNING TO REALLY ENJOY GREEK HISTORY

Dress like a Greek

Instead of running naked through the local woods, you could find out what it was like to be a groovy Greek by dressing like one. Here's a simple groovy costume to make.

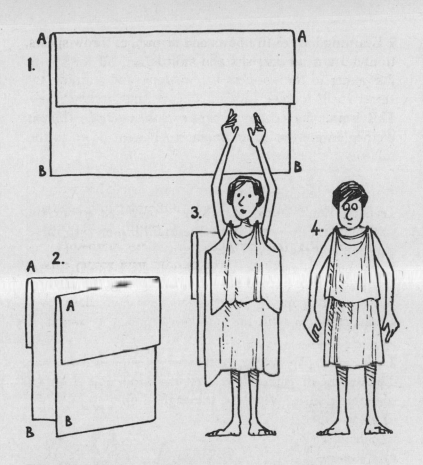

(**Warning:** Only suitable for summer weather.)

1 Fold an oblong cloth as shown – do *not* use Mum's best sheets for this – use Dad's.

2 Fold it again.

3 Wrap it round the body and pin it at each shoulder – the Greeks didn't have safety pins, but you can cheat and use a couple.

4 Fasten the open side with pins. Tie a belt around the waist. See picture 4 . . . here's one I made earlier.

5 You are now ready to be seen in public. Try running around and find out why they took them off for sports and games.

This sort of clothing is known as a *Doric Chiton*. Women's were the same design but it went down to the ankle.

Test your teacher
Teachers don't know everything – they just try to kid you that they do. Test their true brain power with these questions on the groovy Greeks . . .

1 Aristotle the great Greek teacher had a favourite meat. What was it?
a) camel
b) turkey
c) horse liver

2 The great playwright, Aeschylus, is supposed to have died when an eagle flew over his head and dropped something on it. What did the eagle drop?
a) a tortoise
b) a hare
c) a stone

A HARE ON THE HEAD

3 As well as the Olympic games there were games in Isthmia. The winners at the Isthmian games were given a crown as a prize. What was the crown made of?

a) celery

b) rhubarb

c) gold

4 Before clever Aristotle came along, the Greeks had a strange belief about elephants. What was it?

a) an elephant has no knee joints so it goes to sleep leaning against a tree

b) elephants never forget

c) eating elephant meat makes you strong

5 Which team sport did the Ancient Greeks enjoy that we still play today?

a) hockey

b) soccer

c) volleyball

6 The Greek teacher, gorgeous Gorgias, said that 'nothing exists' . . . not even himself. He nearly didn't. He had a peculiar birth. Where was he born?

a) in his dead mother's coffin

b) on a mountain in a snow storm

c) on board a sinking ship

7 The Spartan youths tried out their military training by doing what for their town?

a) becoming secret police and murdering troublemakers

b) mending roads and keeping the streets clean

c) becoming servants in old people's homes and cooking for them

8 How far did the Greek explorer, Pytheas, sail?
a) Britain and the North Sea
b) Crete in the Mediterranean
c) America and the Atlantic

9 The Greeks invented a new weapon in the 4th century BC. They set fire to inflammable liquids then threw them over enemy ships or enemy cities. What is this weapon called?

a) Greek fire
b) Zeus's revenge
c) flaming dangerous

10 A sacred plant was sprinkled on graves. But we don't consider it sacred today. What is it?
a) parsley
b) cabbage
c) garlic

Answers: The answer to every question is a).

- If your teacher scored 0 to 5 they need to go back to school.
- 6 to 9 is pretty good.
- If they scored 10 they probably cheated and read the book before you did.

Test yourself

Now test yourself. See how many answers you can
remember by arranging the
following into
the right order . . .

A	B	C
The playwright, Aeschylus,	invented a new weapon called	hockey
A sacred plant	sailed to	a camel
Aristotle, the great Greek teacher,	died when hit on the head by	an elephant going to sleep leaning against a tree
A Greek sportsman	was born in	a tortoise
A Greek sailor	was sprinkled on graves and called	the secret police
A Spartan youth	enjoyed the team sport called	celery
The Greek explorer, Pytheas,	won a crown made from	Greek fire
The Greek teacher, Gorgias,	believed in	the North Sea
A winner at the Isthmian games	trained in	parsley
An early Greek person	enjoyed meat from	his dead mother's coffin

DIE LIKE A GREEK

What's up, Doc?
The earliest Greek doctor was said to be called Aesculapius. But, since he was supposed to be the son of a god, he probably didn't exist.

But his followers, the Asculapians, did exist. They didn't work from a hospital, they worked from a temple. Most of their patients recovered with rest, sleep and good food. But Asculapians liked people to think they were gods so the patients had to say prayers and make sacrifices.

The temple was famous because no one ever died in the temple of Aesculapius and his doctor-priests! How did they manage this?

They *cheated*. If someone was dying when they arrived then they weren't allowed in. And if they started dying once they got inside they were dumped in the nearby woods.

The doctor-priests were in it for the money. They warned patients that if they didn't pay, the gods would make them sick again. And they advertised. Carvings in the ruins show the doctor-priests made fantastic claims . . .

LAST WEEK A ONE-EYED MAN CAME TO THE TEMPLE. WHILE HE SLEPT THE GODS RUBBED OINTMENT ONTO THE EYELID, HE WOKE UP WITH TWO EYES.

SPECIAL OFFER AT THE TEMPLE—TWO FOR THE PRICE OF ONE

A SPARTAN GIRL, ARETE, SUFFERED FROM WATER ON THE BRAIN. AESCULAPIUS SIMPLY CUT OFF HER HEAD AND DRAINED THE WATER OFF. HE THEN CLEVERLY STITCHED THE HEAD BACK ON

BRILLIANT... UNFORTUNATELY HE STITCHED ON THE WRONG HEAD

NERAMUS OF MYTILENE WAS BALD. HIS FRIENDS MADE FUN OF HIM. WHILE HE SLEPT AESCULAPIUS RUBBED OINTMENT IN HIS HEAD. NERAMUS WOKE UP WITH A THICK HEAD OF BLACK HAIR

JUST REMEMBER TO GIVE IT A BOWL OF MILK EVERY DAY—AND KEEP AWAY FROM MICE

In time, the temples changed into proper medical schools. Later, the great Hippocrates (460 – 377 BC) came along and said that magical cures by the gods were nonsense. He believed in the proper study of the body, and experiments.

Hippocrates was so great that today's doctors still take the Oath of Hippocrates (though it has been modified during the 20th century) and promise, 'I will give no deadly medicine to anyone if asked . . . I will use treatment to help the sick but never to injure.'

Could you take the groovy Greek version of the oath? You would have to swear . . .

But Hippocrates wasn't perfect. He said there were 91 bones in the body – now we know there are 206!

He also believed in 'bleeding' as a cure. A young man with a rumbling tummy was 'bled' by Hippocrates until he hardly had any blood left in his body . . . and he recovered!

One test for a lung disease was to shake the patient – and listen for the splashing inside.

Old Doc Hippo was a bit of a whinger. He complained that, 'If a patient gets worse or dies, people always blame the doctor.'

Still, *you* would complain if you had to do what Hippo had to do. Hippo took samples of . . .

- vomit
- ear wax
- tears
- snot
- pee
- infected wounds

. . . and he tested them. But he didn't test them in a laboratory with chemicals the way modern doctors can. He tested them by what?

1 colour
2 boiling them with rhubarb juice
3 tasting them

AFTER YOU

NO NO AFTER *YOU* DOCTOR

Answer: 3 Either the doctor or the patient had to taste the sample.

95

Hippo and his followers also practised cutting into the skull to drain fluids off the brain. But he wasn't the first to do this . . . there is evidence that Stone Age people did this operation. (Would you like to be operated on by a surgeon with a flint axe?)

The superstitious Greeks kept the piece of bone as a good-luck charm. It was supposed to keep you safe from disease.

But Hippo said some things which doctors today, every day, still say to their patients. . .

Fat people die sooner than thin people.

Hippo also said how doctors should look and behave . .

A doctor must be careful not to get too fat. Someone who can't look after his own fitness shouldn't be allowed to look after other people's.

Secondly he should be clean, wear good clothes and use a sweet (but not too strong) scent. This is pleasant when visiting the sick.

He must not look too grim or too cheerful – a grim man will worry the patient while a laughing man may be seen as an idiot.

And he must have been a good doctor because he lived to the age of 99 years.

Medical monster

Not every doctor was as good and unselfish as Hippocrates. Menecrates of Syracuse was much more grasping and cruel. He was especially fond of really sick patients because he could blackmail them.

Medical manure

Of course, if you didn't want to go to a doctor like Menecrates then you could always try curing yourself. The great thinker, Heraclitus, did this.

He fell ill with dropsy – a disease where you swell up because there's too much fluid in your body. He decided to test his doctors by asking them a riddle. 'How do you make a drought out of rainy weather?' The doctors didn't know the answer – neither do I. Do you?

So Heraclitus decided to cure himself. He reckoned

the best way to get rid of too much liquid was to apply heat. In his farmyard he had a pile of rotting animal droppings – manure. The centre of the manure pile was warm.

Heraclitus buried himself up to the neck in the manure . . . and died.

Warning: Do *not* try this at home. If the manure doesn't kill you, your mother probably will – and your friends won't speak to you till you've had a hundred and five baths.

Perilous plague

One thing Greek doctors could do nothing about was the plague. The plague which killed hundreds in Athens in 430 BC . . .

- probably came from Egypt
- came so suddenly that rumours said the enemies had put poison into the water tanks
- started with a headache and sore eyes
- made breathing difficult and turned the throat red
- made victims begin to sneeze
- caused sickness when the infection moved to the stomach
- caused the temperature to rise so a plague victim couldn't stand wearing any clothes
- made victims grow terribly thirsty so they threw themselves into wells
- covered them in spots
- usually killed the victim
- often caused survivors to lose their memory.

98

Birds of prey wouldn't normally go near the dead bodies as they lay waiting to be buried. The birds that did always died.

The historian, Thucydides, said. . .

> *People died whether they had treatment or not. What cured one person often killed another. Some caught it by nursing others and they died like sheep. In fact this was the greatest cause of death. Corpses lay where they died on top of each other and the dying lurched around the streets and wells in their crying need for water.*

Some families burned their dead. Thucydides also said that passing funerals often dumped their body on somebody else's funeral fire . . . then ran off!

Deadly Docs: 1

King Pyrrhus of Greece had a deadly doctor in 278 BC. The doc wrote to the Romans and said . . .

DEAR FABRICUS,
I AM THE DOCTOR TO PYRRHUS, IF YOU ARE WILLING TO PAY ME I WILL POISON THE KING

But Fabricus sent the letter straight back to Pyrrhus, his enemy, and explained. . .

UNTO KING PYRRHUS, GREETING,
YOU HAVE MADE A BAD CHOICE OF FRIENDS AND ENEMIES, YOU ARE AT WAR WITH HONEST MEN, BUT HAVE WICKED AND UNFAITHFUL MEN ON YOUR SIDE. AS YOU WILL SEE FROM THE LETTER THERE IS SOMEONE IN YOUR CAMP WHO PLANS TO POISON YOU. WE ARE TELLING YOU THIS BECAUSE WE DO NOT WISH TO BE BLAMED FOR SUCH A TREACHEROUS ACTION. WE WISH TO END THIS WAR HONOURABLY ON THE BATTLEFIELD.
FABRICUS

King Pyrrhus found the traitor and gave the doctor a taste of his own medicine, as it were, by having him executed. He was so grateful to the Roman enemies that he set his Roman prisoners free without a ransom.

Deadly Docs: 2

If you can't poison the enemy king then at least you can *stop* him taking medicine that would get him *better*. How? *Tell* him he's being poisoned by his doctor . . . even if he *isn't!*

THAT ASPIRIN WILL MAKE YOUR HEADACHE WORSE

That's what Darius did to his enemy, Alexander the Great. Alexander was sick and received a letter from the double-crossing Parmenio. Like Fabricus's letter, it said . . .

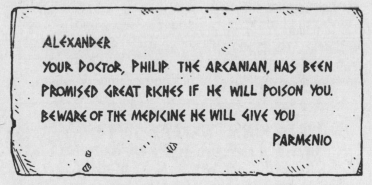

ALEXANDER

YOUR DOCTOR, PHILIP THE ARCANIAN, HAS BEEN
PROMISED GREAT RICHES IF HE WILL POISON YOU.
BEWARE OF THE MEDICINE HE WILL GIVE YOU

PARMENIO

That evening, Doctor Philip arrived with a cup full of medicine. Alexander had the letter by his bedside. Was it really poison in the cup?

Alexander did a brave thing. He handed the letter to Doctor Philip. At the same time he drank the cup of medicine in one swallow.

Philip was impressed. 'But how do you know it wasn't poison?' he asked.

'I don't know about poison,' Alexander told him, 'but I do know about men. And I know you would never betray me, my friend.'

Alexander recovered. Not all doctors were cunning and treacherous.

Medical mystery

Which 'doctor' travelled through time to help the Greeks at Troy? (Clue: He gave them the idea about building a wooden horse.)

Answer: Doctor Who in the 1980s British television series. (Captain Kirk of the Starship Enterprise also popped back to Troy in an episode of *Star Trek;* but Kirk decided not to interfere. Troy must have been full of time travellers and their machines. Strange that Homer didn't mention them in his poems!)

A WOODEN HORSE YOU SAY. THAT'S A MUCH BETTER IDEA. WE WERE GOING TO BUILD A WOODEN HEDGEHOG

ODD OLYMPICS

The groovy Greeks liked nothing better than a contest. The first Olympic contests were simple foot races. The first few Olympics had just one race on one day – a race of about 190 metres or the length of the stadium.

A second race – twice the length – was added in the 14th Olympics, and a still longer race was added to the 15th competition, four years later. But new events were added until the meeting lasted five days. There was even a Junior Olympics for kids.

● The bad news, girls . . . females were banned from the ancient Olympics.

● The bad news, boys . . . clothes were banned for the male athletes.

Choose your champion

You may wish to try an Olympic contest against the class next door. First you need to have a contest in your own class and choose your champion to represent you. Then go and cheer your champion as they compete against rival class champions.

Here's what to do. First choose your judges. They must train as judges (or referees) for ten months before the Olympics. They must also be honest. (You could have a problem finding an honest adult.) Agree the starting time and place and let the competitors battle it out.

● foot race – 200 metres
● double foot race – 400 metres
● standing long jump – with a kilo weight held in each hand to swing you through the air

- quoit-throwing (nearest to a fixed spot wins)
- javelin

After the contest . . .
1 Give the winners crowns made from the branches of a wild olive tree that grows in a sacred grove. (If you can't find one then make cardboard crowns from a sacred cornflakes packet.)
2 Call out the victor's name and country to the assembled crowds. (Or just phone the local newspaper.)
3 When the victor returns to their home they enter through a special gap knocked in the city wall. (Might be better if you *didn't* knock down the school wall. That's there for a purpose – to stop wild pupils escaping.)
4 The victor is treated with special favours – they either pay no taxes, or have free meals at the president's house for life. (Perhaps you could offer your victor a lifetime of free school dinners.)

5 Don't forget to cheer the loser. Losers have feelings too. (An Olympic wrestler called Timanthes lost his strength as he grew older. He was so upset he lit a big fire – then threw himself into it.)

Some groovy Olympic games you might not like to try

Mule-racing – smelly.

Relay – a bit hot. The god, Prometheus, stole fire from the gods and brought it down to earth for humans. But the humans had to escape from the other avenging gods. They ran with torches. The Olympic relay was run with flaming torches instead of batons, in memory of Prometheus. If the torch goes out your team loses. And if you grab the wrong end of the torch from the last runner . . . ouch!

IT'S NOT MY HAND I'M WORRIED ABOUT!

Four-horse chariot race – dangerous. The poet Homer described an accident. . .

Eumelos was thrown out of the chariot beside the wheel. The skin was ripped from the elbows, nose and mouth, and his forehead smashed in over the eyebrows. His eyes filled with tears and his powerful voice was silenced.

A bit rougher than your school rounders match, eh?

Hoplite racing – heavy, but not groovy. Wearing full armour and carrying weapons, this was hard work – try running with a couple of dustbins strapped to your back and that's how it might feel.

HOPLITE, NOT LIGHT HOP!

Trumpeters' competition – deafening.

Pancration . . . what? Pancration was a bit of a mixture of boxing and wrestling. The only rule was that there were no rules, apart from no biting and no gouging out the eyes. Just flatten the opponent. You could . . .

- strangle
- kick
- arm-twist
- jump up and down on your opponent.

Quite good if you're a winner. Painful for a loser.

Boxing – ordinary old boxing? Yes, harmless little fisticuffs – unless you do it the ancient Greek way, as the horrible historical story of Creugas and Damoxenos shows . . .

The Greek Guardian

still only 20 obols

Creugas the Corpse Claims Crown

In the Olympic heavyweight championship yesterday Damoxenos, the Dark Destroyer, beat challenger Creugas . . . and lost the title!

In a sensational contest the two men were both defending their unbeaten records. A crowd of two thousand sat on the grass in the afternoon sunshine to enjoy a fight to the end. They didn't know what an end it was going to be.

Boos

Big Damoxenos was booed as he stepped on to the grass and had leather wrapped around his mighty fists. The handsome Creugas was cheered as he stepped forward. The voice of the referee rang out across the grassy circle.

'Remember, slaps with the open hand, punches with the fist or blows with the back of the hand are allowed. Kicking is permitted, but no head butting. Understand?'

'Yes sir,' Creugas answered boldly. Big Damoxenos just grunted.

'The fight goes on without a break until one man has had enough,' the little ref went on. 'Show you are beaten by raising your right hand in the air. Understand?'

Damoxenos just sneered. 'I'll not need to remember that,' he boasted. 'I'll not be surrendering.'

Hammer

The crowd booed again as the referee stepped back. 'Box!' he cried and Damoxenos lunged forward. He swung his fist like a mighty hammer at Creugas's head but the young man jumped back and flicked a fist at the champion's head.

107

That was the pattern of the fight. Big Damoxenos lumbering round, swinging huge punches but unable to catch the slippery Creugas. Just as the crowd was growing restless, the sun sank down and the referee called a halt.

'We cannot have a draw,' he cried. 'The contest will be decided by a single blow struck by each man.'

First

The crowd seemed to like that and they closed in to get a better view.

'You go first, wimp,' Damoxenos growled. The big man held his arms by his sides – the crowd held its breath.

Creugas struck a hammer blow to the champion's head. The big man just laughed. 'My turn.'

The young man shook his head and waited for the blow that would surely knock him senseless. It didn't.

Instead the big ox hit Creugas cruelly under the ribs with straight fingers. His sharp finger nails tore through the young man's skin. He pulled back his hand and jabbed again. This time he tore out the challenger's guts.

The crowd gasped as Creugas fell lifeless to the ground.

Cheat

The ref ran forward. 'One blow is all that is allowed. You took *two* blows, Damoxenos, you cheat. I hereby disqualify you. I declare that Creugas is the champion!'

The crowd cheered with joy. The new champ was not available for comment.

His manager said, 'The boy done well. Deserved that win. We'll have a few drinks later to celebrate.'

Creugas will always be remembered as a champion who had guts.

Did you know . . .? Olympically speaking

1 There was a fine for cheating. The cheat had to pay for an expensive statue of the god Zeus. And at Olympus there were an awful lot of Zeus statues before the Greek Olympics ended. There must have been a lot of cheats.

2 The main form of cheating was to have a really good set of horses in the chariot race then have a bet that you would *lose* the race. You made sure you lost the race by pretending to whip the horses to go faster . . . while secretly tugging at the reins to slow them up. This 'pulling' of horses to win money still goes on today.

3 The Greek Olympics were banned by the rotten Romans. The Romans didn't much like sport when they conquered the Greeks. The Romans preferred their own groovy 'games' . . . like fights to the death between gladiators . . . and they built huge coliseums to stage the contests. But they let the beaten Greeks keep their Olympics until miserable Roman Emperor, Theodosius, abolished them in 394 AD.

4 The Greek Olympics had competitions in music, public speaking and theatre as well.

5 The Olympics vanished for 1500 years. They were revived in 1896 by Pierre de Coubertin, a young French nobleman, and since then they have been staged every fourth year. The ancient Greek Olympics were held in honour of Zeus, and all wars would cease during the contests. The Olympics came first. Sadly, in the modern Olympics, war came first; the games stopped during World War I and World War II (1916, 1940, 1944).

6 A cook, Coroibus of Elis, was the first recorded winner.

> I THINK I'VE LEFT THE OVEN ON

7 The boy athlete, Pisidorus, took his mum to the Olympics. Because women were banned, she had to be disguised as his trainer.

8 . . . and, talking about trainers. There are quite a few 'Nikes' at modern Olympics. But did you know that Nike was the goddess of victory, who watched over all athletic contests?

9 A sports arena was one 'stadion' (600 Olympian feet, 190 metres) long. That's why we have sports 'stadiums' today. The competitors raced up and down, not round and round.

10 The poet Homer described a race between Odysseus and Achilles. Odysseus was losing and said a quick prayer to the goddess, Athene. She not only made Achilles slip – she made him fall head first into cattle droppings. He stood up spitting cow dung – and lost the race, of course.

HOORAY WELL DONE GOOD MAN

ODYSSEUS GETS A PAT ON THE BACK AND I GET A PAT IN THE FACE!

FUNNY FOOD

Sacrificial snacks

A sacrifice is *supposed* to be a groovy gift to the gods. 'Here you are, gods, here's a present for you. I'm being nice to you, so you will be nice to me, won't you?'

When the Greeks sacrificed an animal to a god, they roasted it and they ate it. That's a bit like buying your mum a box of chocolates then scoffing them yourself.

- The greatest honour was to have some roasted heart, lungs, liver or kidney from the sacrificed animal.
- The best meat was shared around.
- Everything left was minced together and put into sausages or puddings – but the important people didn't bother with those.
- This didn't leave very much for the gods to eat, you understand. Just the tail, the thigh bones and the gall bladder.

The Greeks even mixed the blood and the fat together and stuffed it into the bladder of the animal. They then roasted and ate this little treat. Would you like to try this to see what the Greeks ate? (Without all the mess of sacrificing a cow, of course. That can make a terrible mess on the living-room carpet.) Then go to your local butcher's shop and ask for it. But what do you ask for?

1 haggis
2 black pudding
3 sausage

DON'T YOU THINK YOU'RE TAKING THE SACRIFICE THING A LITTLE TOO FAR?

Did you know . . .?
Vegetarians in ancient Greece wouldn't sacrifice animals to the gods. Instead they sacrificed *vegetables* – groovy, eh?

Munching Milon
Milon was a wrestler. He also thought he was pretty groovy. Before one Olympic contest he walked around the stadium with a live young bull on his shoulders.

He fancied a snack after all that effort, so he killed the bull and ate it. He finished the whole bull before the day was out.

But maybe there are some gods on Olympus with a sense of fair play. Because, in the end, Milon got what he deserved. *Exactly* what he deserved.

It started with him showing off again. He split open a tree with his bare hands . . . but his hand became stuck in the split. Try as he might he couldn't get free. When a pack of wolves came along they licked their chops and moved in on Milon.

What did they do to Milon? Just what Milon did to the young bull – except they probably didn't cook him first.

Foul food
The Greeks ate the meat of sacrifices but didn't eat a lot of meat in their normal day-to-day lives. One historian

112

said, 'The Greeks had meals of two courses; the first a kind of porridge – and the second a kind of porridge.'

In fact it wasn't quite that bad. The 'porridge' was more a sort of paste made up of lentils, beans and corn all ground up with oil – vegetable oil, not the sort of oil garages put in cars.

The peasants had some olives, figs, nuts or goats-milk cheese to add a bit of taste. They washed it down with water or goat's milk.

After about 500 BC the rich started to eat more meat than the peasants – goat, mutton, pork or deer – and drink wine rather than water. But what else did they eat of the following?

Spartan soup

You might not have enjoyed living in Athens and eating grasshoppers and thrushes. But you could have been worse off. You could have lived in Sparta.

The Spartans had a disgusting concoction called Black Broth. They mixed pork juices with salt and *vinegar* into a sort of soup.

The Athenians made some very cruel comments about Spartan food. Athenaeus said, 'The Spartans claim to be the bravest people in the world. To eat food like that they'd *have* to be.'

Another Athenian said, 'It isn't surprising the Spartans are ready to die on the battlefield – death has to be better than living on food like theirs.'

The groovy Greek guzzler

Archestratus wrote the first ever cookery book in Europe. It was written in *verse* and probably meant to be recited at feasts – not used as a recipe book. It contained some quirky bits of advice to eaters and to cooks. Archestratus seemed a rather grumpy man with strong views on some foods . . .

> *A Pontic fish, the Saperde,*
> *Is poor and tasteless and it smells.*
> *To those who eat this thing I say,*
> *Both you and it can go to hell!*

And Archestratus had his own favourite foods. He liked to rubbish more popular dishes . . .

Now some men like the taste of beef,
They sing the praises of the cow.
While I would rather get my teeth
Into the belly of a sow.

But Archestratus saved his nastiest comments for foreign cooks who ruined good Greek food with their recipes . .

If your food you want to waste,
Take a Bass fish from the sea,
Find a cook with awful taste
Like the cooks from Italy.

Syracuse has bad cooks too
Spoiling Bass in sauce of cheese.
Or in pickles, taste like glue,
Keep away from cooks like these.

Just as well he didn't live to taste our modern versions of Italian delights. He might have written a horrible verse like . . .

Spaghetti hoops that come in tins
Belong in deep and dusty bins.
As for tasteless plastic pizza
Simply leave it in your frizza.

GROOVY GREEK GROWING-UP

Bother for babies
From 500 – 200 BC there was a ritual way of treating babies. Would *you* survive?

Father inspects baby. Is it fit?
Yes Go to 1.
No Go to 2.
Don't know Go to 5.

1 If you have too many boys then they'll have to split up your land when you die. Too many girls will cost you money. Do you want to keep it?
Yes Go to 6.
No Go to 2.

2 Put the baby in a pot (a pithos), then leave baby on a hillside to die. Do you care?
Yes Go to 4.
No Go to 3.

3 Baby dies before it's a week old.

4 Let a childless couple know what's going on. They will get to it before the cold or the wolves do. Baby lives with foster parents.
Go to 6.

5 Father will 'test' the baby by rubbing it with icy water, wine or urine (yeuch). Does it survive?
Yes Go to 6.
No Go to 3.

6 The baby is one of the family. Tell the world with an olive branch on the door if it's a boy, a piece of wool for a girl.
Go to 7.

7 Hold the *Amphidromia* ceremony. When baby is seven days old, sweep the house and sprinkle it with water. Father holds baby and runs round hearth with it while family sings hymns.
Go to 8.

8 When baby is ten days old have the naming ceremony. (A boy is named after his grandfather.) Congratulations – you've made it . . . unless disease or plague or war or something else gets you!

The good news: Boys didn't go to school until they were seven – girls didn't have to go to school at all.

The bad news: You didn't add up with numbers. You added up with letters – a = 1, b = 2, c = 3 and so on.

But do you know what number DAD + HEAD make?

Answer: 214 + 8514 = 8728

The really bad news:
Boys took a slave to school with them. No, *not* to do their work. The job of the slave was to make sure the boy behaved himself. If he didn't then the slave would give him a good beating.

117

Test your teacher

The Greeks loved thinking about things – the science of thinking about things became known as 'philosophy'. But it was a thinker from Italy who came up with the most curious thoughts – Zeno of Elea. The Greeks loved talking and thinking about Zeno's 'problems'. Test your teacher with this sneaky (and Greeky) question . . .

Surviving school dinners

Have you ever been to school dinners and seen nothing you fancy? What happens? You go hungry.

The Lydians went hungry for a very long time because there was a famine. They decided to do something about the problem. They discovered that the more you think about food the hungrier you get. So they invented games to take their minds off food. They played dice and knucklebones.

The games were so interesting they didn't notice they were hungry. The next day they ate whatever they could find but didn't play games. This went on for 18 years! Games one day, food the next.

So, if you don't fancy a school dinner then play knucklebones. You need five ankle-joints from *cloven-footed* animals. (They make neat cubes of bone.) There are several cloven-footed animals – bison, pigs, goats, antelopes and sheep. If any of those appear on a school-dinner menu then you might just be in luck.

If your school cook slaughters her own wildebeest in the kitchens, then ask her for the little cube-shaped bones from the ankle joint. If she *doesn't* then you'll just have to use small cubes of wood like dice.

Knucklebones: 'Horse in the Stable'

Players: One or more players.

You need: Five knucklebones (or wooden cubes).

Rules: Put four knucklebones on the ground. Each one is a 'horse'.

Put the left hand near them with the fingers and thumb tips spread out and touching the ground. The gaps between the fingers are the 'stables'.

One knucklebone is tossed into the air with the right hand.

Before catching it the player must knock one 'horse' into a 'stable' with the right hand – that is, they must flick a knucklebone into a gap between the fingers.

With the right hand, catch the knucklebone that was thrown in the air.

Repeat until all four 'horses' are in their 'stables' – no more than one 'horse' to a 'stable'!

If all four are put in their 'stables' then move the left hand away from the 'horses'. Toss the throwing stone into the air with the right hand, pick up all four horses with the right hand, and catch the throwing stone in the right hand.

If the turn ends with a full 'stable', or if the player makes a mistake, pass the turn to the next person.

The first to 'stable' all the 'horses' ten times is the winner!

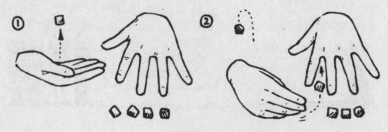

120

The school Olympics

Greek children invented games like knucklebones that are still played in some parts of the world today. In fact you may even have played some of the games yourself. If you haven't, and want to play like a groovy Greek, then here are the rules for six games.

Ostrakinda

This is a game for two teams that is still played in Italy, Germany and France. You need: A silver coin. Paint one side black with poster paint – this side is 'Night'. The plain side is 'Day'.

Rules: 1 Divide into two teams – the 'Nights' and the
'Days'
2 Spin the coin in the air.
3 If it lands black side up then the Nights chase the Days – and if it lands silver side up the Days chase the Nights.

Cooking pot

Rules: 1 Choose someone to be 'It'.
2 'It' is blindfolded and sits on the ground.
3 The others try to touch or poke 'It'.
4 'It' aims to touch one of the teasers with a foot.
5 Anyone touched by a foot becomes 'It', is blindfolded and sat on the ground.

WHERE IS EVERYBODY?

ANYONE TOUCHED BY THOSE FEET WILL *NEED* TO SIT DOWN

Bronze Fly

A sort of Greek Blind-man's Buff. A Greek described it

. . .

> They fastened a head-band round a boy's eyes.
> He was then turned round and round and called out, 'I will chase the bronze fly!'
> The others called back, 'You might chase him but you won't catch him.'
> They then torment him with paper whips until he catches one of them.

ISN'T THAT A BULL WHIP?

Ephedrismos

Rules: 1 A player is blindfolded and gives a second one a piggy-back.

2 The rider then has to guide the player to a target set on the ground.

3 If the player succeeds then he becomes the rider. This could become a competition where pairs race to reach the target.

ARE YOU SURE THIS IS THE WAY TO THE TARGET?

Greecket

The Greeks also played ball games where you throw a ball at a 'wicket', rather like cricket without a batsman.

We just have pictures of these games that have been painted on Greek vases, but we don't have their written rules. Make up your own rules – maybe they played like this . . .

1 Stand on a mark a fixed distance from the wicket.

2 Take the ball and have ten attempts to hit the wicket.

3 The opponent stands behind the wicket (like a wicket-keeper) and throws the ball back to you every time.

4 Then you stand behind the wicket while your opponent has ten tries.

5 The one who has the most hits on the wicket from ten throws is the winner.

6 Try again from a different mark.

It looks (from the vase paintings) as if the loser has to give the winner a piggy-back ride.

Kottabos

Rules: 1 Take a wooden pole and stand it upright.

2 Balance a small metal disk on top of the pole.

3 Leave a little wine in the bottom of your two-handled drinking cup.

4 Grip the cup by one handle, flick the wine out and try to knock the disk off the top of the pole.

(Would you believe grown-up Greeks played this silly game at parties?)

You can try this with a cup and water and a 50p coin on the end of a broom handle . . . but *not* in your dining-room, please.

Puzzle your parents

So your parents think they're smart, do they? Give them this simple test to check their brain-power. All they have to do is answer 'Groovy Greeks', 'Terrible Tudors' or 'Vile Victorians' . . .

Who had these toys or games first? The Greeks, the Tudors or the Victorians?

1 puppets moved by strings

2 draughts

3 tug of war

4 dolls with moving parts

5 model chariots
6 yo–yos
7 babies' rattles
8 spinning-tops
9 see–saws
10 bowling hoops

Answer: All were first played by the *Greek* children. Any other answer is wrong. How did your parents score?

10 probably cheating
6–9 quite good – for an adult
3–5 go back to school – or read 'Groovy Greeks'
0–2 never *ever* let this parent offer to help with your homework. Your pet hamster could do better. In fact a *dead* hamster could do better.

125

THE ROMANS ARE COMING

Bodge-up at Beneventum!

As the Greek armies grew weaker, the Romans grew stronger. At first the groovy Greeks won all the battles – but lost a lot of men each time. The Romans learned from their mistakes and got better every battle, until finally, in 275 BC . . .

AND WORSE WAS TO COME. A YOUNG ELEPHANT WAS MADDENED BY THE ROMAN SPEARS. IT CHARGED AROUND THE BATTLEFIELD LOOKING FOR IT'S MUM. IT ALSO TRAMPLED ITS GREEK OWNERS

MUMMY!

RESULT: ROMAN I - GREEKS AND ELEPHANTS UNITED 0

Jumbo facts

1 The first Greek to come across an elephant army was Alexander the Great when he invaded India.

2 Apart from trampling and terrifying the enemy, elephants gave a good shooting platform for archers.

3 The Greeks used elephants supplied by India. The elephant trainers came with them. The elephants grew from babies with their trainer. No one else could command an elephant because it only understood the trainer's Indian language.

4 An elephant trainer was important to the Greeks and he was paid more than the average soldier.

5 A year after the bodge-up at Beneventum the Greeks arrived at Argos. In the battle an elephant lost its driver. The creature ran round the battlefield until it found him, dead on the ground. It picked him up with its trunk and rested the body across the tusks before carrying its dead master off the battlefield. And it wasn't too bothered who it trampled to death as it crossed the battlefield – Greek friends as well as Roman enemies.

Pathetic Pyrrhus

King Pyrrhus met a particularly pathetic end in his battle to defeat the Romans. In 274 BC he was fighting at the siege of Argos when a peasant with a pike hurt him. The peasant didn't hurt the King very much, you understand, but Pyrrhus was furious and turned to smash the pike man with his sword.

Poor Pyrrhus reckoned without the women of Argos. They had climbed up to the roof tops to watch the battle. They must have been like proud parents watching a school football match. You know, the sort who stand on the touchline and shout things like, 'Get stuck in, our Timothy!' And, 'Come on ref – get your eyes tested!'

Anyway, who should be watching Pyrrhus attacking the pike man peasant? The peasant's mum.

'Hey! That's my little boy you're trying to kill, you big bully!' she cried. The woman tore a tile off the roof and flung it at Pyrrhus.

Well, the woman was either an Olympic-standard discus thrower . . . or very, very lucky. The tile gave Pyrrhus a crack on the back of the neck, just below the helmet. His neck was broken and he dropped dead from his horse.

If there'd been newspapers in those days, *The Argos Chronicle* would have enjoyed that story. Imagine the headlines . . .

PROUD PIKE PEASANT'S
PARENT POTS
PATHETIC PYRRHUS

. . . perhaps?

EPILOGUE

After the groovy Greeks came the rotten Romans. The Romans were supposed to be an even greater people than the Greeks. After all, they eventually ruled over half the world – including Britain.

But the Romans were pretty rotten compared to the Greeks. Their games weren't great sports events like the Olympics – they were just an excuse to watch humans kill animals, animals kill humans, animals kill animals and humans kill humans. In boxing, for example, the Greeks bound their hands with leather bands like boxing gloves. The Romans bound their hands with leather bands – but put vicious spikes in them.

The Greek plays had been exciting and interesting. The Romans tried to copy them but were looking for more action and violence. Roman plays eventually killed people on stage for real.

One story about the take-over of Greece by the Romans gives a good example of what the world lost when the rotten Romans took over from the groovy Greeks . . .

Archimedes was a brilliantly clever Greek. When the Romans attacked his people in the city of Syracuse (211 BC) Archimedes used his great and groovy brain to invent wonderful new weapons.

For two years the Romans were kept out of the city as the inventor created 'death-rays' – giant mirrors that reflected the sun on to Roman ships in the harbour and set them on fire – and huge catapults that drove them off.

But at last the Romans broke through the Greek defences and brought terror to the citizens of Syracuse as they killed and stole from the houses. The Roman commander had given one strict order, however: 'Find Archimedes – but don't hurt the great man.'

At last a Roman soldier burst into Archimedes' house. The inventor was in the middle of an experiment and was too busy to bother with a small matter like an invasion at that moment.

The Roman was puzzled. Why was this old man ignoring him?

The Roman became angry. How *dare* this old man ignore him?

The Roman lost his cool. He killed the defenceless inventor. With one blow he destroyed one of the cleverest men the world has known.

The Roman soldier was punished for disobeying the commander's order not to harm Archimedes. But that didn't bring the old man back. Just as none of even the greatest Roman achievements could bring back the glory of the Greeks.

The rotten Romans ruled – the groovy Greeks went to their graves. That's horrible history for you.

THE ROTTEN
ROMANS

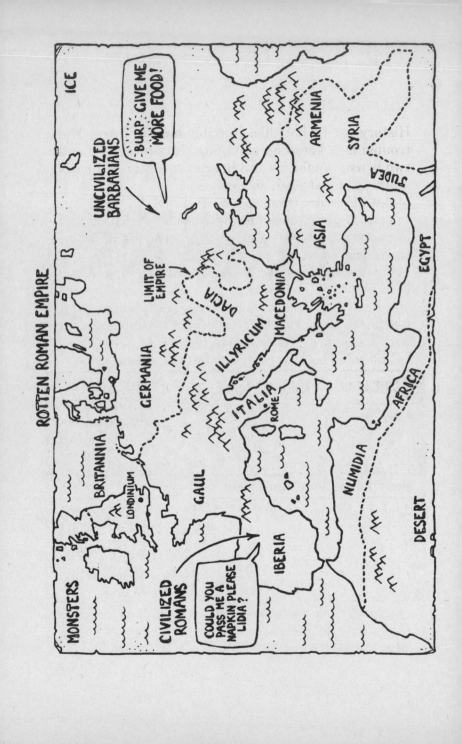

THE ROTTEN ROMANS

Introduction

History can be horrible. Horribly hard to learn. The trouble is it keeps on *changing*. In maths, two and two is *usually* four – and in science water is *always* made up of hydrogen and oxygen.

But in history things aren't that simple. In history a "fact" is sometimes not a fact at all. Really it's just someone's "opinion". And opinions can be different for different people.

For example . . . you probably think your teacher is more horrible than the cold cabbage and custard you had for school dinner. That's *your* opinion. But teacher's mum probably thinks he's sweeter than tea with six sugars. That's *her* opinion.

You could both be right – or both be wrong . . .

See what I mean? Both right, both wrong!

Of course, honest answers like these don't get you gold stars. No! Teachers will try to tell you there are "right" and "wrong" answers even if there aren't.

There are worse things than horrible history. Want to know what? Teachers' jokes are more horrible than the Tower of London Torture Chamber ...

So, history can be horrible. But when you find the real truth about the past you can suddenly discover it's horribly fascinating. Everyone loves a good murder story – history is full of them, like the murder of Julius Caesar. Blood all over the place.

And there are war stories, thrillers, horror stories and comedies. That's the sort of history you'll find in this book. With a bit of luck you might even horrify your teacher!

TERRIBLE TIMELINES

The rotten Romans' timeline

BC

753 Roman *legend* says Rome was founded by Romulus. The *truth* is that the early Romans were farmers living in a region called Latium.

509 The Romans are fed up with their cruel king, Tarquin. They throw him out and rule themselves (that's called a Republic).

264 First of the Punic Wars against the great enemy, Carthage (in North Africa). Result: Rome 1 Carthage 0.

218 Hannibal of Carthage attacks Rome with the help of elephants. He can't capture Rome but rampages round Italy terrorising people.

202 Scipio takes charge of the Roman Army and beats Hannibal. Rome 2 Carthage 0. The Roman farmers take over more and more land till they have the whole of Italy.

146 Third War to wipe Carthage out forever. Game, set and match to Rome! The Romans get to like the idea of conquering people! They start on the rest of the world.

130 By now the Romans have conquered Greece and most of Spain.

100 Julius Caesar is born.

59 Julius Caesar becomes Consul for the first time.

55 Julius Caesar invades Britain for the first time because (he says) **a)** the Belgae of south Britain are helping the Gauls of north France to rebel against the Romans, and **b)** there is a wealth of tin, copper and lead to be found in Britain.

44 Julius Caesar is elected dictator for life – then murdered!

AD

43 Claudius gives orders for the invasion of Britain . . . again!

60 One tribe, the Iceni, rebel. Queen Boudicca leads them in massacres of Romans. Roman

General Paulinus defeats her and she poisons herself.

80   Julius Agricola completes the invasion (except for the Picts in Scotland).

84   Agricola beats the Picts at Mons Graupius in Scotland.

122   Hadrian starts building a wall across northern England to keep out the Picts.

235–285   Fifty-year period with over 20 Roman emperors mainly because they keep getting murdered.

313   Emperor Constantine allows Christian worship.

380   Christianity becomes official religion of Rome.

401   Roman troops are being withdrawn from Britain to defend Rome.

410   Barbarian tribes from Germany begin attacks on the empire and Rome itself.

476   The last Roman emperor of the western empire is forced to retire.

1453   The empire of the east falls to the Turks. End of the Roman Empire.

The battling Britons' timeline

BC

6500   The Ice Age ends, the sea level rises. The north-west corner of Europe is cut off by the sea. The British Isles are formed. The islanders are Britons.

3600   The Britons build Stonehenge.

2150   Tin is discovered in the south-west. Mixed with copper it makes the hardest metal yet known to humans – bronze.

900   Britons make human and animal sacrifices at Peterborough.

600   Iron takes over from bronze for making weapons and tools.

70   Druids are becoming powerful leaders of the Britons.

55   Julius Caesar invades but doesn't stay for long.

AD

10   Britain independent from Rome but some British leaders like to copy Roman way of life.

138

30 The rich south-east of Britain under one ruler – Cunobelinus – who gives himself the Roman name of "Rex", meaning "King".

41 Cunobelinus dies; his sons Togodumnus and Caratacus take over. They're not so keen on the Romans.

42 Verica (king of the Atribates in southern England) is thrown out by his people because he is friendly with Rome. (Caratacus was stirring them up!) Verica flees to Rome and asks for Roman help.

43 The Romans invade and Togodomnus is killed after a battle at the River Medway.

51 After years of resistance Caratacus is betrayed and handed over to the Romans in chains.

60 Queen of the Iceni in East Anglia, Boudicca, leads a rebellion against the Romans and is defeated. The Romans also destroy the Druid sanctuary in Anglesey.

122 Emperor Hadrian's wall is begun, to stop the Picts and Scots invading England.

125 Britons are encouraged to join the Roman Army – and become Roman citizens when they retire.

213 *All* free Britons become Roman citizens – but Roman citizens pay Roman taxes!

367 As the Roman Empire weakens, the attacks on Hadrian's Wall increase.

405 As the Romans leave, their way of life leaves soon after – Roman coins are replaced by the ancient custom of bartering.

410 The Emperor Honorius tells the Britons, "Defend yourselves," as the Irish, the Picts, the Scots and the Saxons (from north Germany) begin to raid Britain.

420 Saxons begin to settle in eastern Britain.

443 Plagues in the towns help drive people back to the old British ways of country living.

446 The British appeal to Rome for help against the Saxons. No help arrives. The days of Roman Britain are over. The Saxons have the rich south-east. The Britons have to make do with the poor, wild north and west.

140

KEY

1 DAMNONII	6 PARISI	11 DEMETAE	16 ATREBATES
2 VOTADINI	7 ORDOVICES	12 DOBUNNI	17 BELGAE
3 SELGOVAE	8 CORNOVII	13 CATUVELLAUNI	18 CANTIACI
4 NOVANTAE	9 CORITANI	14 TRINOVANTES	19 REGNENSES
5 BRIGANTES	10 ICENI	15 SILURES	20 DUROTRIGES
			21 DUMNONII

THE ROTTEN ROMAN ARMY

The Roman Army didn't run all of Roman Britain. Once they'd won the battles they moved on to fight somewhere else. Towns were built in the conquered territories with Roman lords in charge. Just in case the Britons felt like revolting, the Romans let retired Roman soldiers settle in the land outside the towns – a circle of trusted men to warn of danger. And, if the beaten Brits *did* give trouble then the army could get back quickly to help by marching along the new Roman roads.

Your teachers will tell you all about the legions and what they wore and how they lived. But they don't know everything.

Test your teacher . . .

Ask your teacher these questions. Can they get more than 5 out of 10? Can you?

If you were a Roman soldier . . .
1 What would you wear under your leather kilt?
a nothing

b underpants

c fig leaves

2 Where would you drive on the Roman roads?
a on the right
b down the centre
c on the left

3 How long would you have to stay in the army once
you joined?
a 25 years
b 5 years
c the rest of your life

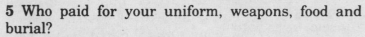

4 Who could you marry?
a anyone
b no one
c a Roman

5 Who paid for your uniform, weapons, food and
burial?
a the emperor
b they were free
c you paid for them yourself out of your wages

6 How tall did you have to be?
a over 1.8 metres
b between 1.6 and 1.8 metres
c under 1.6 metres

7 What would you use instead of toilet paper?
a a sponge on the end
of a stick, dipped in
cold water
b your tunic
c the daily newspaper

8 Your spear (pilum)
had a 60 cm metal
head that would snap
off after it hit something. Why?
a so the enemy couldn't pick up the spear and throw
it back
b so you could put the metal head in your pocket
when you were marching
c because the Roman armourers couldn't make the
heads stay on

9 Why was one Roman Centurion called "Give me another"?

a because he liked his soldiers to sing as they marched. When they'd finished one song he'd call out, "Give me another!"

b because he was greedy. After eating a pig's head he'd cry out, "Give me another!"

c because he cruelly beat his soldiers so hard he smashed his canes and had to call out, "Give me another!"

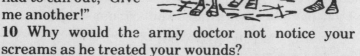

10 Why would the army doctor not notice your screams as he treated your wounds?

a because he enjoyed making you suffer

b because he was trained to carry on without paying attention to a soldier's cries

c because the Romans only employed deaf men as doctors

Answers: 1b. 2c (But they often barged straight down the middle of town streets in their chariots. They marched there too, trampling anyone who got in the way with their hob-nailed boots!). 3a. 4b (But they often had wives outside of the camp). 5c. 6b (But this rule was sometimes broken when the army was desperate for men . . . and the men who were too small might still have to work for the army even if they couldn't fight). 7a (And you'd share it with everyone else in the public toilets! Sometimes you'd use a lump of moss, though, and that would be flushed away). 8a. 9c. 10b.

The rottenly clever Roman Army

The Romans were the best army in the ancient world because they used something their enemies didn't. The Romans used their brains! Are you as brainy?

Here are some problems the Romans overcame. What would you have done if you'd faced these problems . . .

1 Julius Caesar had a land army in Gaul (northern France). When the Veneti tribe there rebelled, they captured two Roman messengers and sailed off with them. Caesar quickly had ships built and followed. The Veneti were excellent sailors but poor fighters. Caesar needed a weapon that would stop the Veneti ships from sailing off while Roman soldiers climbed aboard. There was no gunpowder (for cannon or bullets). What simple (but very successful) weapon did the Romans make?

2 After the British Queen Boudicca was beaten, the Romans were able to move into the fenlands of East Anglia. The grass was rich but the land was very wet. If the Romans tried to wade through the swamps, the local tribes ambushed them. Then a new general arrived from Italy's Pontine marshes. He showed the soldiers how to get through swamps without wading up to their waists in water. What did he teach them?

3 In the early days of the Roman Republic, the Romans came up against the Greek king, Pyrrhus. The Greek strategy was to go into battle led by elephants. The elephants would charge at the Romans, trample them and send them running. But the Romans learned quickly. At the battle of Beneventum they found a way to face an elephant charge . . . and win! What would *you* do?

4 Some of the young men in the conquered lands did not want to fight in the Roman Army. It meant leaving their homes, farms and families to fight (and maybe die) in some distant corner of the world. The young men cut off the thumb of their right hand so they couldn't hold a sword. If they couldn't hold a sword then they wouldn't be expected to fight in the Roman Army. The Roman generals realised that all of these thumbless young men were trying to outwit them. What was their solution?

5 One day, Emperor Hadrian went to the public baths where his skin was carefully cleaned by slaves with scrapers. He saw an old man rubbing his back against a column. The old man was one of Hadrian's old soldiers. Hadrian asked why he was rubbing himself against the marble. The old man said it was because he couldn't afford a slave with a scraper. Hadrian gave the man slaves and money. BUT . . . next day the public baths were full of old men rubbing their backs against the marble! They were obviously scrounging for a Hadrian handout! What would you do if you were Hadrian?

146

Answers:

1 The Romans attached hooked knives onto the ends of long poles. As they neared the Veneti ships, the Romans slashed the enemy ropes and sails to stop them sailing. They then climbed aboard the Veneti boats and overpowered the sailors. The leaders were executed and the sailors sold for slavery.

2 How to use stilts! They were a great success at first. Eventually the tribes of the fens learned to knock the Romans off the stilts and stab them as they fell. Ah, well, it seemed like a brilliant idea at the time!

3 The Roman front line split in two. The elephants charged harmlessly through the line. They were too clumsy for the drivers to stop and turn. The helpless riders just kept going to the back of the Roman Army, where there were special troops waiting with long, sharp spears. They jabbed the elephants until the maddened creatures turned round and charged back again. The elephants flattened the Greek army, who weren't expecting them!

4 Cut off their heads! Anyone trying to avoid army service was sentenced to death. The young men soon learned this new law and decided to fight – possible death in war was better than certain death by execution. The Romans also branded or tattooed unwilling soldiers – if the soldier deserted, then he would have trouble hiding the fact that he was supposed to be in the army.

5 Hadrian simply told the old men to rub each other!

Make the punishment fit the crime

If you think punishments at school are hard, then how would you like to have been in the Roman Army? The barbarian armies charged at the Romans like bulls at a matador – and we know who usually wins *that* contest. The Roman Army had "discipline". They did what they were told, every time. And if they didn't do as they were told – no matter how small the offence – they had to be punished. Try to guess which crime earned which punishment . . .

CRIME	PUNISHMENT
I LAZINESS	A. DECIMATION OF A UNIT – I MAN *IN* EVERY X IS EXECUTED
II FALLING ASLEEP ON DUTY	B. SLEEP OUTSIDE THE SAFETY OF THE CAMP
III RUNNING AWAY IN A BATTLE	C. GET THE WORST FOOD – ROUGH BARLEY INSTEAD OF GOOD CORN
IV PUTTING YOUR UNIT IN DANGER	D. DEATH BY BEATING
V RUNNING AWAY WITH YOUR UNIT	E. DEATH BY STONING

Answer: 1B. 2C. 3D. 4E (Your unit would throw the stones). 5A ('The unlucky one in ten was chosen by drawing lots).

Let the reward fit the action

Of course there were *good* sides to being a Roman soldier too – otherwise no one would have wanted to join the army! The goodies were . . .

1 The army took two parts of every seven you earned in wages and saved it for you. When you retired they gave you all your savings and a piece of land. You could retire in comfort . . . if you lived long enough.

2 You could make extra wealth by robbing the countries you defeated. You could take money, animals or even living prisoners that you could sell for slaves.

3 For brave actions there were no medals – there were crowns:

a a crown of oak leaves – for saving the life of a fellow citizen (Caesar won one at Mytilene when he was just 20 years old)

b a crown of plaited grass – for rescuing an army under siege

c a crown of gold – for being the first soldier over the wall of an enemy town

149

Don't get sick!

Roman doctors knew how to . . .

AMPUTATE MANGLED LIMBS
REMOVE TONSILS
MEND BROKEN BONES

NEXT!

BUT – Roman doctors didn't know about anaesthetics (to put you to sleep while they hacked you about!).

Roman doctors could make medicines to cure sickness.

BUT – they had to mix them with honey to try to disguise the disgusting tastes.

Did you know?

A Roman legionary always went into battle with a first-aid kit of bandages and healing herbs?

THE CUT-THROAT CELTS

The Britons were part of the Celtic peoples. At one time the Celts had roamed round the world as much as the Romans did. One man put an end to all that – the Roman emperor, Julius Caesar.

The Celts used to fight fiercely for their tribal chiefs. But the tribes often fought *against* each other when they should have been fighting *together* against Julius Caesar. They needed one strong leader to bring them all together. But when that leader arrived it was too late.

Vercingetorix was a Celtic chief who was just as clever as Caesar at fighting and leading. Would you have been as clever as Vercingetorix? Here are some of the problems he faced. Could you have solved them?

151

Vercingetorix v Caesar

1 You meet the chiefs of the tribes every day to plan your war against Caesar. One of the chiefs argues against you. What do you do about him?

a Say to him, "Look, my friend, we must all stick together if we want to beat the rotten Romans. So, please, trust me. Remember, united we stand but divided we fall."

b Get upset. Say, "If you're going to argue with me you can find yourselves another leader. I'll fight Caesar by myself. When I've beaten him I'll beat you next. You'll be sorry!"

c Don't get upset. Simply have his ears cut off and one of his eyes gouged out. Send him back to his tribe with the message, "This is what you get if you mess with Vercingetorix!"

2 Caesar is a long way from home and a long way from fresh supplies. The Romans need food for the soldiers and their horses. They are getting it from the Celtic towns in the region of the Bituriges tribe. What can you do to stop them?

a Tell the Bituriges' chief to burn his towns to the ground and send his people to live with other tribes.
b Tell the Bituriges' chief to destroy all the food in the towns but let the people stay.
c Tell the Bituriges' chief to burn his towns to the ground but move all the people to the capital city of Avaricum.

3 Your tactics are working. Caesar is getting desperate for food. He sets off for Avaricum, which is the region's grain depot. How can you defend Avaricum against Caesar's army?
a Build a wooden wall.
b Build a stone wall with a ditch in front.
c Build a brick wall.

4 Caesar begins to build towers on wheels to push up to the walls. When these towers reach the walls the Romans will let down a drawbridge at the top and swarm over your walls. What can you do?
a Build an even taller tower behind your walls and throw down fireballs on top of them.
b Leave the town and attack Caesar's towers.
c Run away.

153

5 Caesar cannot get the towers near the walls because there is a ditch in front of the walls. He sends soldiers into the forest to chop down trees. He rolls the logs into the ditch and begins to fill it up.

What can you do to stop the Romans filling the ditch?

a Dig a tunnel under your walls and set fire to the logs?

b Surrender.

c Send a raiding party out to steal the Roman axes so they can't chop down any more trees.

6 The Romans manage to get towers up to the walls. You would like to set fire to them but the clever Romans have covered them with leather, which doesn't catch fire very easily. What can you throw at them instead?

a dead horses
b boiling fat and tar
c cold water.

7 Despite your efforts the Romans reach the walls. They catch hold of the top of the wall with hooks, and swarm up the ropes attached to the hooks. What's the best defence against this?

a Throw the hooks back.

b Pull the hooks up and drag them inside your fort.

c Wait for the Romans to climb them and try to kill them as they reach the top.

8 During the Roman assault it begins to rain heavily. What do your defenders do?

a Run for shelter until the rain stops and hope the Romans do the same.

b Fight on and get wet.

c Ask the Romans for a cease-fire until the weather improves.

9 The Romans reach the streets of Avaricum. They begin slaughtering every man, woman and child in sight. What should Vercingetorix do?

a Give himself up.

b Fight to the death.

c Make sure his best fighting men escape through a back entrance.

10 Vercingetorix reaches the safety of Alesia. The Romans are following. You have a large army. What should you do with it?

a Send most of the army away to gather help from other Celtic tribes and keep just a few to defend Alesia.

b Keep all the soldiers in Alesia and hope that help will arrive.

c Leave the army in Alesia and go for help yourself?

155

Vercingetorix's ten steps to Rome, or, Answers:

1 Vercingetorix could not afford to show any weakness or he'd be killed by the other Celtic chiefs. He could not plead (**1a**) or sulk (**1b**). He had to show he meant business and would make an example of anyone who opposed him (**1c**).

2 Vercingetorix made just one mistake. He couldn't destroy the supplies and leave the people in the towns (**2b**) – the warriors would not have fought if they knew the Romans had captured their wives and children. He should have destroyed the supplies AND the towns (**2a**). If you chose **2a** then you'd have been a crueller but better leader than Vercingetorix! But the Bituriges were proud of Avaricum. They pleaded with Vercingetorix not to destroy it. He weakened and agreed (**2c**). From then on he was pretty well doomed.

3 Vercingetorix had fought the Romans for years and knew their way of fighting. They would have simply burned a wooden wall (**3a**) and battered down a brick wall (**3c**). The best wall was a solid stone wall with a ditch in front (**3b**).

4 Caesar wasn't put out by the solid walls of Avaricum. He began building towers. Vercingetorix expected this and didn't give up (**4c**). Of course, he didn't leave the safety of the town and attack the Romans in open battle (**4b**) because that's exactly what they wanted. He just ordered bigger towers to be built behind his own walls (**4a**).

5 Caesar could defeat the ditch by filling it with

new logs. Vercingetorix couldn't stop him (**5c**) but didn't let it beat him (**5b**). The Bituriges were good iron miners and so could dig shafts. They dug one under the Roman logs and set fire to them (**5a**). This delayed the Roman attack . . . but failed to stop it.

6 The Celtic soldiers knew that the only thing that would slow down the Roman towers wasn't anything solid (**6a**), but liquid, which would run through the joins in the Roman "umbrella". Cold water wasn't going to hurt them (**6c**) but boiling tar and oil would. This is what they did (**6b**).

7 The Romans were determined – and getting hungrier! They began to use grappling hooks to climb the walls. There was no point in throwing them back (**7a**) because the Romans would just try again at another spot. No one had been able to stop the Romans by trying to kill them at the top (**7c**) because there were just too many of them. Clever Vercingetorix devised the plan of hauling up the hooks and taking away the Roman weapons (**7b**)!

8 When a rain-storm hit Avaricum, all of Vercingetorix's cleverness was undone by the stupidity of his men. They should have fought on (**8b**). The Romans wouldn't let some rain stop them (**8c**) and it was no use expecting them to. The defenders ran for shelter (**8a**). The Romans leapt over the walls.

HEY! WHERE DID EVERYBODY GO?

9 Vercingetorix knew that the battle for Avaricum was lost, but the war wasn't. He wasn't going to give up (**9a**). On the other hand there was no point in waiting to be killed (**9b**) when there were new Celtic armies waiting to fight. All he had to do was to escape with the soldiers and fight again (**9c**). Unfortunately, the women who were being left behind to be massacred didn't like the idea. Not surprising really! They began wailing and screaming. This gave the escape plan away to the Romans and they hurried to cut off the escape route. The Romans massacred 40,000 Avaricum people. Only Vercingetorix and 800 others escaped to fight another day.

10 Vercingetorix reached the safety of Alesia with a new large army. If he'd tried to keep the army with him (**10b**) they'd have eaten the supplies in no time and starved to death before help arrived. He couldn't get to all the dozens of tribes himself to get help (**10c**) so he sent his troops to different Celtic tribes and kept just enough to defend the town (**10a**).

It almost worked. A huge Celtic army arrived. But the Romans had built a ring of defences round the town. The soldiers in Alesia couldn't get out. The new Celtic army couldn't get in. They gave up and went away.

Vercingetorix was trapped. He gave himself up to his own people and said they could do what they needed. The Romans wanted Vercingetorix alive – that was how the Celts delivered him. In 45 BC he was paraded through the streets of Rome . . . then executed. The Celts on the continent were crushed. They survived mainly in the islands off the shores of Europe. The British Islands. If Caesar wanted to finish them off, then he had to invade Britain . . . which he did.

That's why it's thought that the defeat of Vercingetorix led to the Roman invasion of Britain! If Vercingetorix had only destroyed Avaricum (as in **2a**) then we might never have had a Roman Britain!

Heads you win, heads you lose

Heads were popular with the Celtic race to which the Britons belonged. Here are ten horrible brainless facts . . .

1 In 500 BC, the British tribespeople believed that the head had magical powers. They thought that severed heads could utter prophecies and warnings, especially if they were in groups of three.

2 Rotting human heads were stuck on poles at the entrance to a hill fort.

3 Heads could be thrown into a lake or river as a gift to the gods.

4 After a battle the Celts rode from the battlefield with the heads of enemies dangling from the necks of their horses.

5 The heads might then be nailed to the walls of their houses.

6 Sometimes they were preserved in cedar oil and taken out years later to show off to visitors. A Roman visitor said that the Britons would not part with their lucky heads for their weight in gold.

7 The Celtic Boii Tribe of the Po Valley (Northern Italy) took skulls and covered them in gold. They would then be used as cups!

8 Heads featured in many ornaments of stone, metal or wood and paintings. Severed heads could be seen staring at you from the surface of tiles, pots, sword hilts, chariot fittings and even bucket handles!

9 Because the gods were more powerful than humans, they often had more heads. An Irish goddess, Ellen, had three heads! The druids had to keep her constantly supplied with sacrifices to stop her coming out of her underworld cave and ravaging the land.

161

10 The Britons even told stories about the magical power of the head. Many legends involved severed heads.

A typical story is the Welsh legend of Bran the Blessed . . .

DAILY HEADLINE NEWS

HEADITOR : M.T. SKULL

BIG BRAN'S NOGGIN NICKED!

Some treacherous troublemaker has taken Britain's greatest treasure!

Yesterday the London burial place of Bran the Blessed was robbed. The great warrior's head was later found to be missing, along with another two skulls from the graveyard. The authorities are looking for a man with three heads!

Magical

As all our readers will know, the head of Bran the Blessed was the most magical article in the whole of Britain. Eighty years ago Bran was mortally wounded in a bloody battle with an Irish king. As he lay dying he ordered the seven surviving soldiers to cut off his head and carry it with them. This they did and they found themselves in the afterlife as the guest of Bran – even though they weren't dead!

Then one warrior disobeyed one of Big Bran's orders. He opened a forbidden door. The warriors were heaved out of heaven. But, before they went, one of them tucked Bran's head up his tunic. And so it returned to earth. The head was buried in London, where it would guard Britain against evil for ever more.

Reward

Now it has been stolen there's no knowing what might happen. *The Daily Headline News* is offering a reward for information leading to its return. Otherwise Britain will be heading for disaster!

163

Did you know?

The Romans sometimes treated slaves brutally in their conquered territories and in Rome itself. In AD 157 the Roman writer Apuleius described life in a rotten Roman flour mill . . .

The slaves were poor, skinny things. Their skin was black and blue with bruises, their backs were covered with cuts from the whip. They wore rags, not clothes, and hardly enough to keep them decent. They had a brand mark burned into their forehead and half of their hair was shaved off. They wore chains around their ankles.

A slave revolt was led by Spartacus at a gladiator school near Naples. The slaves formed a huge army and terrorised the area for a couple of years. At last a Roman army defeated them. Over 6000 slaves were crucified along the side of the main road from Capua to Rome.

YOU JUST CAN'T GET THE STAFF THESE DAYS

THE BATTLING BRITONS

If you weren't a Roman then the Romans called you "barbarian" – or stranger. This was because the Romans didn't understand the language of strange peoples. They said they sounded like sheep – "bah-bah-bah" people . . . bah-bah-rians . . . barbarians, get it?

So, when the Romans arrived in Britain they met "barbarians". But the Britons weren't "barbarous" – they weren't rough, crude, simple people. They were simply "different". Still, they *did* have one or two habits that you won't find in your school today . . .

The British way of life . . . and death

1 The Britons had priests called Druids. Druids led the worship of the gods of Nature. An important time of year was Beltane – 21 March – when night and day are exactly 12 hours each. If people wanted the days to keep getting longer, and summer to come, then they had to give the gods something they would like. The Druids thought that the gods would like nothing better than a severed head . . . so the Druids had a victim's head chopped off.

2 The Britons lived in forts with huge earth walls. They built one called Maiden Castle in the south of England. The Britons would feast there on joints of pork. They got rid of the bones by throwing them over their shoulders. When the piles of bones became too deep, they levelled them out and spread a fresh layer of earth and chalk over the top.

3 The men wore long moustaches which trapped food as they ate. A fussy Roman writer called Diodorus wrote, "Their drink passes through their moustaches like a strainer!" Yuk!

4 At a British tribal feast the guests would sit on animal skins on the floor, eat with their fingers . . . and keep on eating! When they were tired, they just rolled over onto the skin carpet and fell asleep.

5 The Britons weren't as filthy as they sound from this. They used to wash with soap long before the Romans did.

6 In battle, Celtic warriors often fought without any clothes at all. The Romans said that the Britons were painted from head to toe in a blue dye called woad ... but maybe they were just blue with the cold!

7 The Celts believed in staying thin and fit. If a young warrior became too tubby for a normal sized belt then he was fined.

8 The Britons were related to the Celtic tribes of Gaul (northern France) who were feared by the Romans for their fierceness. And not only the men! Marcellinus said . .

> *A whole troop of foreigners would not be able to withstand a Gaul if he called for his wife to help him. Swelling her neck, gnashing her teeth and swinging her white arms of enormous size she begins to strike blows mixed with kicks as if they were missiles sent from the string of a catapult.*

9 The Celtic men were proud of their hair. They bleached it by washing it in lime. The roots of the hair would be dark and the rest a bleached blond. The lime also made the hair stand on end. They went into battle with their hair in a crest of spikes. One writer said the spikes were so stiff and strong that you could have stuck an apple on the end of each point! And they didn't wear helmets that could save their life in a battle – it would have spoiled their hairstyle!

10 Brave British women must have looked as fearsome as their blue warrior men. They painted their fingernails, reddened their cheeks with a herb called ruan and darkened their eyebrows with the juice of berries.

But the boldest of British women – maybe the bravest ever – was Queen Boudicca.

That was what the Britons called her. Later generations changed her name to Boadicea. Some people say this change was made because Boadicea sounded nicer. Another story is that a mediaeval monk made a spelling mistake when he was copying an old history and his mistake was copied by later historians! Let's call her Boudicca . . .

Boudicca, *This is Your Life!*

1 Boudicca always looked pretty fearsome with her huge mop of bright red hair, her rough voice and her king-sized body. A Roman writer, Cassius Dio, said . . .

> She was very tall. Her eyes seemed to stab you. Her voice was harsh and loud. Her thick, reddish-brown hair hung down below her waist. She always wore a great golden torc (band) around her neck and a flowing tartan cloak fastened with a brooch.

BOUDICCA

2 She married Prasutagus, King of the Iceni tribe of Britons. They had two daughters. Prasutagus, the wimp, didn't fancy fighting the Romans when they arrived. Instead he tried to make a deal with the emperor: "When I die the Iceni lands can be split between you and my daughters." Then he did a stupid and wimpy thing – he died.

3 The Roman Army simply took over. The officers ran the country while the slaves plundered the Iceni houses. Then the Romans made a BIG mistake. They had Big Boudicca whipped. Big Boud was not amused.

4 The Romans had whipped Boudicca . . . so Boudicca whipped up a rebellion. The revolting Britons captured the Roman town of Camulodunum (now called Colchester in Essex).

5 The gods appeared to be on Big Boud's side. They gave the Brits several "signs" that they were on the side of the Iceni.

- The Roman statue of Victory fell down . . . face down as if it were fleeing from the attackers.
- Women reported that ghostly, ghastly shrieks could be heard in the Roman senate house and theatre.
- At the mouth of the Thames, a phantom town was seen in ruins.
- The sea turned blood red.
- As the tide went out, the sands took on the shape of corpses.

6 Big Boud marched on to Londinium (London) and Verulamium (St Albans) where her army did a lot of murdering and pillaging. In all they killed about 70,000 people.

7 One Roman didn't run away. Paulinus had just 10,000 soldiers to fight 100,000 Brits.

8 Big Boud rode round the Brit tribes in her war chariot and gave them her famous speech . . .

We British are used to women commanders in war. I am the daughter of mighty men. But I am not fighting for my royal power now . . . I am fighting as an ordinary person who has lost her freedom. I am fighting for my bruised body. The gods will grant us the revenge we deserve. Think of how many of us are fighting, and why. Then you will win this battle or die. That is what I, a woman, plan to do. Let the men live as slaves if they want. I won't!

9 The 10,000 Romans were well organised. The 100,000 Britons charged around the way they always did. The result was a great victory for the Romans.

10 Big Boud faced another flogging. The Roman historian, Tacitus, said she took poison and died. The Roman historian, Dio, said she died of a disease. Believe whichever one you like . . . or neither. Perhaps she just died of a broken heart. Boudicca, that was your life!

Did you know?

The Roman historian, Tacitus, said the Britons had 80,000 warriors killed in Boudicca's final battle. That means each of the 10,000 Roman soldiers killed (on average) *eight* Britons! He claimed that only 400 Romans died so it took 250 Britons to kill just *one* Roman! No wonder the British lost!

Of course, the fact is that Tacitus was telling *fibs*. He wanted to tell the Roman world what a great army the Romans had and how brave their leaders were . . . after all, his father-in-law was one of those fighting in that battle!

So, DON'T believe everything you read in your history books. If the Brits had been able to write then, they would have given a very different account of the battle. The Romans were very good at blaming other people for things. The truth is usually that there are good arguments on both sides . . .

173

Who's to blame for Boudicca's battles?

SHE SIMPLY SLAUGHTERED ALL THE PEOPLE SHE FOUND IN THE ROMAN TOWNS. THEY KILLED THE WOMEN AND CHILDREN AS WELL

THE ROMANS HAD TAKEN ALL THE RICHES OF PRASUTAGUS AND TURNED HIS RELATIVES INTO SLAVES- WOMEN AND CHILDREN TOO

COWARDLY BOUDICCA ONLY ATTACKED *UNDEFENDED* TOWNS

THE ROMANS WRECKED THE *UNDEFENDED* BRITISH TEMPLES, SMARTY PANTS

OF COURSE, THE BRITISH PRIESTS HAD HELPLESS PRISONERS KILLED IN WALES, SMELLY-KNICKERS

BEFORE YOU GET YOUR TOGA IN A TWIST REMEMBER, THE ROMAN RELIGION WAS AN INSULT TO THE BRITISH GODS

175

Diary of disaster

One of the great heroes of the British tribes was Caratacus of the Catuvellauni tribe (north-west of London). While many tribal leaders were making peace with the Romans, Caratacus went on fighting. In the end he was defeated, of course. But he was still a hero.

That was one big difference. The Romans loved winners. The Britons seemed to love losers. The other difference was that the Romans learned from their mistakes. The Britons didn't.

It isn't likely that Caratacus could write. But, if he could, and if he kept a diary, would it have looked like this . . .?

Summer of 43 AD Kent

Disaster! I can't believe it! After two days of battle the Romans have defeated us. All we had to do was to stop them crossing the ~~River~~ River Medway. There's only one bridge over the Medway. All we had to do was sit tight on the northern end, wait for the Romans to cross it, then cut them into pieces...

... We'd have killed them in their thousands. We would! But what did they do??? They cheated!!! They sent troops upstream, they crossed where the water was shallow and attacked us from the back. That's not fair, is it?

Of course, we could have run them down with our chariots. We could! But what did they do? They cheated again!

They shot our horses. That's not fair, is it? They even killed my brother, Togodumnus. Poor, stupid Toggy. He should have done what I did. Retreated. Like dad always said, "He who fights and runs away, lives to fight another day".

So, I'm alive and next time I'll stuff those rotten Romans!!!!

Late Summer of 43 AD - Dorset

Disater! Again! The Romans are marching west. They're taking our hill-forts one after another. Of course, they don't fight fair. ~~Re~~ They don't fight man to man ~~to~~ and let us kill them....

No. They shoot at our defenders with iron-tipped arrows. Hundreds at a time from some big machine. They drive us off the walls then swarm in after we've taken shelter.

They've taken 20 hill-forts that way. I never thought I'd live to see the day they'd take the mighty Maiden Castle. In fact I nearly didn't live to see today! I just managed to retreat in time. He who fights and runs away.... But I'll stay in England. They'll never drive me into Wales.. Never!!

The other leaders are all surrendering, making peace and getting fat. But they won't get a hero like me. Not like they got poor old Toggy... ~~Net~~ Next time I'll get them...

Summer of 48 AD - Wales

Who is the greatest British leader??
Caratacus. Me! Alright, so I'm stuck in the
wild, wet Welsh mountains. But every now and
then I lead a raid on some Roman troops
and crack a few rotten Roman heads.

Actually it's rather hard to crack a Roman
head. They wear these metal helmets. That's not
fair, that's not. Some people might even call
it cheating!

They'd like to drive me up to North Wales
and into the Irish Sea. Well, there is absolutely
NO chance of that. My men will fight to the
the death (Not my death of course. They
need me alive to lead them)

I'll end up in North Wales over my warriors'
dead bodies!!!

North
Wales

Nth England

Welsh
Mountains

Dorset

Kent

North Wales - 51 AD

Disaster! Again!!! I never thought I'd see the day when the Romans would take a fort like Llanymynech. But they did. I still can't believe it. They couldn't attack Llanymynech from the back because that's a steep mountain face. They couldn't attack it from the front because that's the river Vrynwy and the front wall of the fort

But they did it! They crossed the river then came to the wall. We were pouring spears and stones and ~~and~~ arrows down on their heads. We should have massacred them...

So, what did they do? They cheated, as usual. They put their shields over their heads and came close together. The shields formed a solid wall over them. (They copied this from a Roman animal with a shell called a "tortoise" or something)

Our weapons just bounced off their "shell" and the Romans just kept coming till everyone was captured. The rotten Romans even took my family! I was lucky to escape. He who fights and runs away...... Still, next time I'll get them. I'm going to join forces with Queen Cartimandua of the Brigantes up near York ...

..... They're the biggest tribe outside of Roman rule. With _me_ to lead them we'll chase the Romans all the way ~~to~~ back to Rome. And they can take their tortoises with them.

I even hear old Claudius brought some huge grey monsters called ele_phant_s with him. They can take them back too!!! This time next year I'll be in Rome!!!

North England - later in 51 AD

Life with Queen Cartimandua is great! I don't even miss my poor captured family. The beautiful Carti obviously fancies me. Can't blame her really Me being the greatest British hero ever seen.

Loads of food. Better than living like an outlaw in the hills. And loads of wine. Lovely stuff. The very besht Roman wine. I wonder where she gets it from?

And she's even decorating me with chains. Chains on my wrists. Chains on my ankles. I fink that Carti loves me ~~too~~ show mush she wantsh to keep me here forever!!! I'm very shleepy now.

Nighty night Carti dear!

Next day

My head hurts. And worse. Much worse
I'm a prisoner. I've found out where that
treacherous, ugly, vicious, lying Queen gets
her Roman wine from. She gets it from
   the Romans!!! And what does she give
the Romans in return?

   Me!   I've been handed over to the Romans.
They're taking me back to Rome. It's curtains
for Caratacus! I said I'd be in Rome within
a year, I never thought it would be in
   chains. It's a disaster! They'll execute
me for sure. Me the greatest living British
hero. I'm not afraid to die of course... I just
don't want to be there when it happens.
   ·······

Next week - middle of the English Channel

I think I'm going to be sea-s...

Next month - Rome

What a place! These Romans really know how to treat a hero! Met old Claudius the emperor. Messy little weedy fellow. Dribbles and slobbers and limps about the place. But a very powerful man. Most important man in the world I reckon. And he spoke to me! (I didn't understand a word, of course, because he was blabbering away in Latin. But I could tell he <u>was</u> pleased to see me!)

Claudi gave an order and my chains were cut off. I thought, Aha! This is it! ~~You're~~ You're for the chop, Caratacus. But no! They treated me like a hero. They even said I was free to live in Rome. I think I might just do

that. There are huge buildings all made of stone and marble. I've never seen anything like it.

Who wants to live in cold wet Britain in a draughty wooden hut? Not me! After all, I am the greatest British hero ever. I reckon I've earned an easy life with my old mate Claudi. Maybe the rotten Romans aren't so rotten after all !!!

183

The diary might be imaginary but the facts are about right. Caratacus arrived in Rome and told the Romans that they could only have great victories if they had great warriors (like himself) to fight against. "If you execute me, then all your glory will be forgotten," he warned them. Claudius agreed and released him.

But Caratacus was still puzzled when he saw the wealth of Rome. "When you Romans have all this, why do you want our poor huts?" Good question.

Meanwhile, back in Britain, the treacherous Cartimandua stayed in power (with Roman help) for another 15 years. Then her husband attacked her and kicked her out. The Romans really did take the British forts with ease. The Romans made mistakes. But they didn't usually make the same mistake twice. That's what made them so successful.

Test your teacher

"Please sir/miss/gorilla-features! Where is Boudicca's body now? Is it . . .
a Under her statue on Westminster Bridge (opposite the Houses of Parliament),
b Under platform 8 of King's Cross Station,
c Somewhere at the bottom of the Thames?"

Answer: b Archaeologists believe they have located the grave of Big Boud under Platform 8 of King's Cross Station. However, British Rail rebuilt that platform in 1988 and aren't too keen to have it dug up again to find out if the archaeologists are right. But if you're ever standing on Platform 8 of King's Cross and a big, red-haired woman asks you, "What time's the next chariot to Camulodunum . . . ?"

Did you know?

A mysterious funeral ceremony took place near London in the second century AD. A grave has been discovered in an underground room but it contains no human bodies. There are just two carvings of men who look like Roman senators. Historians think that these men must have died during fighting and were buried elsewhere. It seems that they did not have an honourable burial . . . maybe they were traitors. Whatever the reason their carved heads were walled up in this room to be forgotten. But one body was found in the tomb – the body of the family cat!

185

ROTTEN ROMAN LEADERS

Julius Caesar was one of the greatest Roman leaders. He was so successful he was murdered . . . by his friend! Rome had been run as a "republic" for many years. That is to say the important people in Rome decided what to do. Then Julius Caesar became so powerful there was a fear that he'd take over. The people thought he wanted to become "King of the Romans".

The last king they'd had was a disaster. His name was Tarquinius Superbus who lived in the 5th century BC. He abolished certain rights of Romans and was the rottenest Roman of the time.

Was it true that Caesar wanted to be crowned king? And would he get to be as bad as Tarquinius? If so, it would be better to kill him now! This is how it happened . . .

Caesar's sticky end

1 Caesar had himself elected "Dictator for life" . . . that was just another way of saying the dreaded word "King"!

2 Caesar started wearing red boots! Only a king wore red boots.

3 At a festival, Mark Antony, Caesar's friend, offered Caesar a diadem – a small crown. Caesar took it off – a sign that he didn't want to be king, perhaps? The crowds cheered when he took it off. But did Caesar and Mark Antony set this up to find out how the people felt? What if the people had cheered when the crown had been put *on?*

4 Caesar was due to speak to the Senate (the Roman parliament) on 15 March, 44 BC. Straight after his speech he was due to lead his troops into battle. During a war he'd be surrounded by his soldiers. No one could kill him then. If he was to die then he had to die on 15 March.

5 Caesar was a great believer in "fate" – if he was going to die then there was nothing he could do to change his fortune. A fortune-teller told Caesar not to go to the Senate on 15 March. It didn't stop him.

6 Caesar's wife asked him not to go to the Senate that day. She'd had terrible nightmares and a feeling that something bad would happen. That didn't stop him.

7 Caesar felt ill on the morning of 15 March and was almost too ill to attend the Senate . . . he was worse by the time he left!

8 The killers chose Brutus as their leader. Brutus was one of the most popular men in Rome. He was famous for being honest. If he led the killing then the people of Rome would know the murderers were "honest" – that they did it for the good of the people.

9 On the evening of 14 March someone asked Caesar, "What sort of death would you like?" Caesar answered, "A sudden one." He got his wish.

When Caesar entered the Senate the senators all stood up as a sign of respect. Some of Brutus' gang slipped behind Caesar's chair while others came to meet him. Cimber grabbed Caesar's robe with both hands and pulled it from his neck. This was the signal for the attack.

Casca struck the first blow. His knife made a wound in Caesar's neck, but not a serious one, so that Caesar could still turn around, grab the knife, and hold on.

The watchers were horrified. They didn't dare run away or help Caesar or even make a sound.

Each assassin bared his dagger now. They all closed in on Caesar in a circle. They pushed him this way and that, like a wild beast surrounded by hunters.

Brutus stabbed Caesar in the groin. Above all Caesar had trusted Brutus.

Some say Caesar defended himself against all the rest – but when he saw Brutus coming at him with a dagger, he pulled his robe over his head and sank down.

The attackers pushed Caesar against the statue of his old enemy, Pompey. The statue became drenched with blood.

Caesar received 23 wounds.

Many of the assassins wounded each other as they fought to stick so many knives into one body.

188

The killers made one big mistake. They didn't kill Mark Antony at the same time. "Honest" Brutus said it would be wrong. They were only out to stop wicked Caesar from becoming king. But it was Mark Antony who led a campaign of vengeance that destroyed the killers. Brutus committed suicide when he was defeated by Mark Antony at Philippi in 42 BC.

Caesar had left most of his fortune to his grand-nephew, Octavian. Young Octavian became the sort of dictator that Caesar wanted to be. The thing the Romans feared – rule by one all-powerful man – had returned. And some of the emperors that followed were a hundred times worse than Julius Caesar!

In fact, some of the Roman Emperors were pretty weird. Here are the Rottenest Romans of all . . .

Emperor Tiberius

Ruled: 14 AD–37 AD

Favourite saying: "I don't care if they hate me . . . so long as they obey me!" (Know any teachers like that?)

Nastiest habit: Breaking the legs of anyone who disobeyed him.

Rottenest act: Tiberius needed a holiday. "I think I'll take a break!" he announced. As the servants scuttled off to find their shinpads he cried, "A holiday, I mean. A short break on the island of Capri off the south coast of Italy would be very nice."

He had only been there a few days when a humble Capri fisherman caught a large crab and a huge mullet fish. The poor man decided that it would make a wonderful gift for the visiting emperor.

The cliff was steep and there was no track. The mullet was heavy. The fisherman struggled for an hour and finally reached the top.

"Take me to the emperor," he pleaded with the guard.

"The emperor wishes to be left alone today," the guard said, shaking his head.

"It's the biggest mullet I've ever caught!" the fisherman said proudly. "The gods meant it for the emperor. Tell the emperor I must see him!"

The guard shrugged. It was a boring life, standing

on the top of the cliff watching the gulls. The emperor might order him to break the fisherman's legs. "I'll see what the emperor says," he smirked.

Five minutes later he returned and said with a grin. "The emperor will see you now."

The poor little man dragged the huge fish into the emperor's room. "You'll be sorry," the guard muttered.

As the fisherman stepped through the door two huge guards grabbed his arms. "I've brought a gift for the emperor!" he squeaked.

Tiberius stepped forward. "You disturbed my rest, you smelly little man!" he snarled.

"It's the fish, your worship!" the fisherman cried.

"No!" the emperor jeered. "That fish smells sweeter than you. Guards!"

"Sir?"

"Sweeten the little man. Rub that fish over his body!"

"It was a present . . . ouch! Mullet scales are very rough!" he screamed.

The guard scrubbed the rough skin over the fisherman's face till the skin was scraped off and his face left raw and bleeding. The guard smiled as he stripped the skin off the fisherman's chest.

"Ahh! Oooh!" the man wailed.

"Enough!" the emperor snapped. The guards let the fisherman fall to the floor where he lay groaning and muttering something through his bleeding lips.

"What did you say?" Tiberius growled.

"I just said thank the gods I didn't bring you that big crab I caught this morning," the little man burbled.

The emperor's eyes lit up with evil glee. "Go to this man's house and fetch the crab," he chuckled.

The guard nodded. As he left the emperor's room he winked at the sobbing fisherman. "I told you that you'd be sorry."

And after being scrubbed with the sharp shell of a crab the little man was so sorry that he wished he'd never been born.

Sticky end: Tiberius died at the age of 78, probably suffocated by his chief helper. The Roman people went wild with joy!

Caligula

Ruled: 37 AD–41 AD

Favourite sayings: To his friends at a banquet, "It has just occurred to me that I only have to give one nod and your throats will be cut."

To the guards of a row of criminals, "Kill every man between that one with the bald head and that one over there."

To his people, "Rome is a city of necks just waiting for me to chop."

To everyone who would listen, "I am a god."

Nastiest habit: His little "jokes". At a sacrifice ceremony he was given a hammer which would knock out the beast to be sacrificed. The priest was waiting to cut the beast's throat. Caligula hit the priest over the head instead!

Rottenest act: Caligula loved to organize huge killing festivals with loads of spectators. There were fights to the death between gladiators, and fights with wild animals. But the wild animals had to be kept alive until the day of the contest. Caligula was shocked at the cost of the raw meat needed to feed the animals. So he found a cheap supply of meat . . . he fed criminals to them!

Daftest act: He made his dear friend Incitatus a consul – so Incitatus became one of the most powerful rulers in the Roman Empire. So? So, Incitatus was his favourite *horse!*

Sticky end: One of his trusted guards stabbed him to death. Others went to the palace where they killed his wife and child.

Claudius

Ruled: 41 AD–54 AD

Favourite saying: "K-k-k-k-k- . . . er . . . execute him!"

Nastiest habit: Watching criminals being tortured and men being executed by being flogged to death.

Rottenest act: Claudius discovered his wife was a bit of a flirt and had wild parties with her friends. Claudius not only had *her* executed but 300 party friends went too.

Sticky end: His niece, Agrippina, poisoned him with mushrooms.

Nero

Ruled: 54 AD–68 AD

Favourite sayings: He played the lyre very badly but people told him he was brilliant. The Greeks were particularly creepy about telling him he was good. "Only the Greeks are worth my genius," he would say.

When he knew he had to die all he could say was, "What a loss I shall be to the art of music!"

Nastiest habit: Murdering people. He had his half-brother, Britannicus, poisoned. (Actually, Britannicus had a food taster who ate and drank a tiny bit of every dish that the Emperor was going to eat. If the food was poisoned, the taster would die first. The taster drank some hot wine and passed it over to the emperor. The taster was fine. The wine was "safe" to drink. But Britannicus complained that the wine was too hot and ordered water to cool it. *Then* he drank it . . . and died. The cold *water* had been poisoned!)

Nero had his first wife, Octavia, murdered. Her head was sent to Nero's new girlfriend, Poppaea. But then he murdered Poppaea, too.

Nero had Christians persecuted cruelly . . .

- They would be tied to a post, covered in tar and set alight.
- They would be covered in animal skins and thrown to hungry, wild dogs.
- They were crucified in large numbers.

195

Rottenest act: Agrippina had poisoned Claudius and now her son, Nero, was emperor. She thought she could rule the empire through her weak and wicked son.

Nero had other ideas. His mother was always interfering – stopping his meeting with his girlfriend, Acte, because she wasn't royal. Agrippina had to go.

First he made up their row over Acte. Then he invited mum to join him at a party on the Bay of Naples. Agrippina was happy to accept, glad to be friends with her son once more.

Nero sent a boat to pick her up. A special boat with special oarsmen. For the boat was designed to fall apart at sea and the oarsmen were instructed not to let Agrippina return alive. The boat set off on a beautiful starry night.

But the boat didn't fall apart. There were heavy weights on the wooden canopy over Agrippina's seat. At the right moment they were to crash through the canopy, kill Agrippina and fall through the bottom of the boat to sink it. Everyone would say the boat hit a rock. Sad accident. Poor Nero, losing his loving mother.

That's what was *meant* to happen. But, when the weights fell through the roof they killed Agrippina's friend. Agrippina and her other friend, Aceronnia, escaped . . . and the boat didn't sink!

The oarsmen tried to rock the boat to capsize it. That's when Aceronnia did a very brave thing. She began to cry out, "Save me! I am Agrippina, the emperor's mother! I am Agrippina!"

And in the darkness the oarsmen believed her. They battered her to death with their oars while the real Agrippina slipped over the side and escaped back to her palace. She sent a message to Nero saying what a lucky escape she'd had.

Nero was furious. He decided to make sure the next time. He sent two murderers to her palace. Agrippina thought they'd come from Nero to find out if she was all right!

As the first one battered her with a club she realised her mistake. When the other drew his sword she bared her stomach and invited him to stab her where the ungrateful Nero had come from. He did.

Nero reported that she had killed herself!

Sticky end: When he knew that the Roman Army had deserted him and rebels were coming to arrest him, he placed a sword to his throat. One of his friends gave him a push. The arresting officer arrived as he bled to death.

Ten funny facts about Roman emperors

1 Emperor Caligula's real name was Gaius. Caligula was just a nickname meaning "little boot". This was because he liked dressing up and playing at being a soldier from a very early age.

2 Caligula wanted to copy Julius Caesar and invade Britain. In 40 AD he went to the Roman base in Boulogne (in northern France) where he set sail to lead the invasion. He turned back when he saw that no one wanted to follow him!

3 Augustus Caesar was one of the more human emperors. But even he had his moments – the murder of Julius Caesar really upset him. As Suetonius said, "Augustus showed no mercy to his beaten enemies. He sent Brutus' head to Rome to be thrown at the feet of Caesar's statue."

4 Julius Caesar gave us our modern calendar. The early Romans had 12 months plus a 13th month that was added every four years. In 46 BC Caesar gave us the 12-month, 365-day year with the 29-day February leap year.

5 Emperor Heliogabalus enjoyed the hobby of collecting cobwebs . . . by the ton!

OF ALL MY BELGIAN COBWEBS THIS IS MY FAVOURITE

6 Honorius loved chickens. His favourite chicken was called Rome. He was hiding in his country mansion, safe from the invading army of Goths. When the city of Rome was overrun by Alaric and his army of Goths, a messenger arrived to say, "Rome is lost!" Honorius was heart-broken . . .

until someone told him the messenger meant the capital *city* and not the *hen*.

7 Nero enjoyed the cruel "circuses" so much that he had to take part. He was dressed in the skins of wild animals and locked in a cage. The human victims were tied to stakes in the arena. Nero's cage was opened. He leapt out and attacked the victims.

8 When Emperor Pertinax was murdered there wasn't just *one* person to take his place. *Two* men claimed the throne. Both men thought it would be useful to have the support of the emperor's praetorian guard – so they tried to outbid each other for it. Julianus won. He made an offer of 25,000 sesterces (Roman money) to each man. Unfortunately he couldn't afford to pay *all* the men in *all* the Roman armies across the world. They attacked and threw him out after just 66 days on the throne. The money he spent on bribing the emperor's guards was wasted – they were easily tricked into giving up their weapons.

9 In the 50 years between 235 AD and 285 AD there were about 20 emperors. Most of them were there a short time, murdered and replaced by the murderer who was murdered and replaced by the murderer, and so on. Some of the senior Romans refused to become emperor at this time – not surprising really!

10 Septimius had particularly nasty family problems. He had two sons, Caracalla and Geta. Caracalla was allowed to become joint emperor when he was just 13. Caracalla had his father-in-law murdered, then set off with his father and brother to conquer Scotland. During the campaign, Caracalla threatened to kill his father – but didn't. Old Septimius died in York and his dying words to his sons were, "Do not disagree with each other." Fat chance. Within a year Caracalla had brother Geta murdered. Caracalla was sole emperor at last. He kept the throne for five years, then . . . no prizes for guessing what happened to him. Yes, he was murdered.

Did you know?

Julius Caesar passed burial laws for the inhabitants of new towns built in the Roman Empire:

- "No one may bring, burn or bury a dead person within the boundaries of the town."
- "No crematorium shall be established within half a mile of a town."

(Burial sites had to be either outside the city walls or just within its limits. Caesar wanted a perfect town full of grand buildings and fresh air for his faithful followers.)

ROTTEN ROMAN CHILDHOOD

Children had a tough time in the age of the rotten Romans from the moment they were born. One writer, Soranus, described how each new-born child was laid on the earth and allowed to cry for a while before it was washed and clothed. Only the fit survived.

Some of the Germans in the Roman Empire gave their new-born children an even worse test. They dunked the child in cold water. If the baby came out purple with the cold or shivering then it was a weakling – it wasn't worth bringing up, so it was left to die!

BACKSTROKE?

Girls were named after eight days – boys on the ninth day. Girls would usually take their father's name – but change the "-us" on the end to "-a". So the daughter of Julius became Julia, the daughter of Claudius was Claudia, Flavius was the father of Flavia and so on.

Children would probably have "pet names" or nicknames. One girl was known as "Trifosa" – that means "delicious"!

The Celt names had their own meanings . . .

- Boudicca meant "Victory".
- Cartimandua meant "White Filly".
- Grata meant "Welcome".

Then, if you survived your birth and you could live with your name, you had to face the terrors of the rotten Roman schools . . .

Suffering schoolchildren – the good, the bad and the awful

Good: Schools cost parents money, so only the parents who could afford it sent their children. If you were poor you could miss going to school altogether.

Bad: Slave children didn't go to school. They were born slaves and belonged to the master.

Awful: Poor children missed school but had to work twice as hard for parents. If you didn't your parents might just decide to sell you! It was illegal to sell free children as slaves – but this didn't stop poor parents from doing it. There was not much chance of their being caught.

Good: Education was divided rather as it is today into primary, secondary and college.

Bad: Most children only went as far as primary.

Awful: For laziness in primary school you'd get the cane, or a beating if the teacher didn't have a cane handy. One poet described his bullying teacher like this . . .

His mouth's no good – but he has a hard fist. Why doesn't he become a boxer instead?

WHO ELSE FORGOT TO DO THEIR HOMEWORK?

Good: Primary schools usually had just 10–12 children.

Bad: That was not enough to pay a teacher's wage. So the poor teacher had another job – maybe in a workshop.

Awful: The Romans didn't have the figure zero. That made sums rottenly difficult to teach. Ask your teacher, "Can you add LXXXVIII and XII?" (The answer is "C")

Good: At least schoolchildren had their own goddess. Her name was Minerva. The holiday for the goddess was in March. After the holiday the school year began.

Bad: Each child had to provide their own wax tablets and stylus (sharp pen to scratch letters into the wax), their pen and ink, their paper rolls and abacus (counting frame).

Awful: For a serious offence in the secondary school – a flogging with a leather whip while other pupils held you down.

Good: Schools closed every ninth day for the market – it was probably too noisy to teach on market days.

Bad: Primary schools were pretty boring. You'd study mainly the three 'Rs' – reading, 'riting and 'rithmetic.

Awful: At secondary school you had to study mega-boring grammar and literature, with some geography and, of course, horrible history! By the time you got to college you had to study for public speaking – the Romans believed that good talkers made good leaders. (Do you agree?)

203

A grim life for girls

Through most periods of history it's been harder being a woman than being a man. It was no different in Roman Britain . . .

1 Roman girls were lucky . . . if they lived! "If you give birth to a boy, look after it – but if it is a girl then let it die!" (Letter from Hilarion to his wife.)

2 Men weren't happy with the idea of an educated woman. "I hate a woman who reads", wrote Juvenal in the 1st century AD.

3 Roman women had to be "controlled" from an early age. They were given a lucky charm at birth. Why? Because they didn't have a man of their own to protect them. When a baby girl was eight days old she was taken to a special ceremony. A gold or leather heart was hung around her neck. She would keep it throughout her childhood.

4 When a Roman girl was 14 she was ready for marriage. Who said so? Her father. A husband would be chosen for her. Who chose? Her father. What if the girl didn't like her father's choice? Bad luck. She'd have to marry him anyway.

5 On the evening before the wedding a special event took place. The girl placed all her toys and childhood clothes on the altar of the Lares – the household gods. She also took off her lucky charm – she had a husband to protect her now.

6 The bride always wore a white woollen tunic. It was held at the waist with a woollen belt tied in a special knot. She wore a bright yellow cloak and sandals. Her head was covered with a flame-coloured veil.

7 Roman women wore make-up. They used chalk to whiten their necks because a pale skin was supposed to be a sign of beauty.

8 If a woman's lips and cheeks weren't red enough then they would use a reddish earth called ochre.

9 Women were expected to remove hair from their legs as well as from under their arms. They rubbed hair off with a stone or used a cream to dissolve it – and it's a wonder the creams didn't dissolve the skin too! One hair-remover consisted of the blood of a wild she-goat mixed with sea-palm and powdered viper. Then, if you wanted to stop the hair growing back again, you would have to rub on the blood of a hare.

10 If a girl's eyebrows weren't dark enough then she might have used a metallic stuff called antimony. No antimony? Then girls used ashes! Imagine walking around with mud on your face, chalk on your neck and ashes on your eyebrows. If you got carried away you'd look more like a scarecrow.

Rotten Roman stories

The Romans knew some pretty rotten stories. Stories of gods, graves and guts. Their own gods were a bit boring. But then they heard the stories of the Greek gods. Those gods were much more like interesting people. So the Romans pinched the Greek legends and made them their own. Stories like that of Prometheus . . .

The Eagle has landed . . . again . . . and again . . . and again . . .

The fat, feathered fiend landed on the rock and looked at the man who lay chained to it. The bird's beak was as hooked as a hairpin. His great golden eyes glinted in the harsh sun. "Cor! Stone the crows! What a tasty sight!" he croaked. If he'd had lips he would have licked them. Instead he licked his beak.

The young prisoner lifted his head wearily. He was a handsome young man with nothing on but a loin cloth. He squinted through the fierce sun and glared at the bird. "Push off," he snapped.

The bird hopped from one hot foot to the other. "Hey! That's no way to speak to me! I'll have you know I'm an eagle – king of the birds!"

"Sorry, I'm sure," the man sneered. "I should have said, 'push off, your highness'."

The eagle shrugged. "No need to be offensive. I'm only doing my job. And a bird's gotta do what a bird's gotta do!"

"And I'm tired of every sparrow on Mount Olympus stopping off here to gawp and stare," the prisoner spat.

The bird breathed in deeply and ruffled its breast feathers importantly. "I am here on a mission. Some old geezer at the top of the mountain sent me."

"The *gods* live at the top of the mountain," the man said.

"Yeah, well some old *god* sent me, then. Big guy with long white hair and a bushy great beard."

"Zeus!"

"Bless you . . . anyway, he said, 'Fly down there and you'll see young Prometheus chained to a rock,'" the eagle went on.

"That's me! You've brought me the news that the great god Zeus has forgiven me? I'm to be set free?"

"Nah! The old guy told me to fly down here, and eat your liver."

HELLO LUNCH

"Eat my liver?" the young god groaned.

"Well, I didn't argue, did I?" the eagle chuckled. "I like a nice bit of fresh liver. Specially when its fried with a few onions."

"You'll kill me!" Prometheus cried.

"Nah! You're immortal. You'll 'liver' long time yet! Heh! Heh! Heh!" the bird cackled.

The god blinked as sweat ran into his eyes. "You'll hurt me," he sniffed.

"Can't be helped," the bird croaked and took a step towards his victim. "You must have done something pretty bad to deserve this!"

Prometheus sighed and looked towards the sun. "Once I could move through the air, just like you. One day I flew up to the sun itself. I brought its fire back down to earth."

"Good thing too – otherwise I'd have to eat your liver raw," the eagle chuckled nastily.

The young god went on, "I gave it to the humans to use."

"Sounds fair enough to me," the eagle admitted.

"Ah, but Zeus had told me *not* to give fire to the humans. He was furious. My punishment is to be chained to this mountainside.

"And to have your liver eaten," the eagle reminded him.

"Must you?" Prometheus groaned.

"Cor, stone the crows. You're supposed to be a hero, ain't you? Well, stop whingeing and let me get me dinner."

The bird lunged forward and Prometheus screamed.

When it was over the bird gripped the dripping liver in its talons and opened its wings. The mountain air lifted it gently off the mountainside and the eagle soared upwards. "See you tomorrow, Prommy!" it cried.

"Tomorrow!" Prometheus screamed. "What bit of me are you going to eat tomorrow?"

"Same again!" the eagle cawed. "That's the worst bit of the punishment. Your liver grows back. I'll come back tomorrow and eat it again . . . and the next day . . . and the next . . . until the end of time! Bye for now!"

Prometheus twisted his head to look at his side. There wasn't a mark to show the eagle's work.

And every day the eagle returned. Day after day,

month after month and year after year. Until one day . . .

"Hello there, Prom!" the eagle called happily as it clattered down onto the sun-warmed rock.

"Hello, Eddie," Prometheus grinned.

The eagle took a step back. "Er . . . you look happy this morning, Prom!"

The young god nodded happily. There was a gleam of pure nastiness in his eyes. Suddenly his hand shot forward and he grabbed the bird around its thick neck.

"Awk!" it squawked. "Your chains!"

"A friend of mine came along and snapped them for me," Prometheus smiled and his grip on the eagle's neck tightened. A huge man stepped from behind the rock. He had muscles that rippled like waves on the sea. "Meet Hercules. The greatest hero ever to walk the earth."

"Pleased to meet you, Herc!" the eagle gasped. "Er . . . if you'll just let me go, Prom, I'll get off back to me nest."

"You're going nowhere," Prometheus promised.

"Nah! I was getting sick of liver anyway," the big bird said weakly.

"Hercules is going to kill you," Prometheus said calmly.

"Look Prommy . . . mate . . . old pal . . . there was never anything *personal*, you know! I was only doing my *job!* Stone the crows, a bird's gotta do what a bird's gotta . . ."

His words were choked off with Prometheus' tight hand. He ignored the eagle's words. "But before I let Hercules kill you, guess what I'm going to do?"

"Er . . . me liver?" the bird guessed.

Prometheus nodded.

"Aw, no, Prommy. It'll taste really nasty – yeuch! Honest! Really sour."

"Ah, but you're forgetting one thing, Eddie. There's nothing in this world that tastes so sweet as . . . revenge!"

Did you know?

The founders of Rome, Romulus and Remus, were supposed to have survived being left to die on a hillside. A she-wolf adopted them. When they grew up, Romulus killed Remus and created Rome – named after Romulus, of course. If he hadn't, then this book might have been called, *The Rotten Remans!*

210

ROTTEN ROMAN FUN AND GAMES

Rotten Roman games

Which of the following modern games do you think the Romans had?

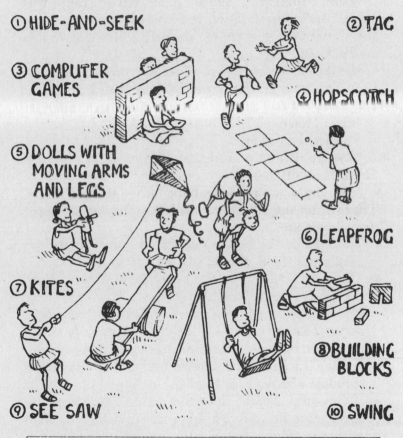

① HIDE-AND-SEEK

② TAG

③ COMPUTER GAMES

④ HOPSCOTCH

⑤ DOLLS WITH MOVING ARMS AND LEGS

⑥ LEAPFROG

⑦ KITES

⑧ BUILDING BLOCKS

⑨ SEE SAW

⑩ SWING

Answer: all except 3

Some Roman games you might like to try

Roman children's games were a bit like ours . . . only rottenly vicious at times!

Trigon

- Next time your parents slaughter a pig for dinner, ask them for the bladder – it's a part you won't be eating anyway.
- The bladder is cleaned out, then blown up like a balloon and tied.

- A triangle with sides about two metres long is drawn on the ground and a player stands at each corner of the triangle.
- The bladder-ball is passed from one player to another without it touching the ground.
- The aim of the game is to keep the bladder-ball in the air as long as possible.
- Easy? Then add two more balls so that each player has one. There is no set order for passing the ball. You may have to pass your ball while receiving two from the other players! (Game hint: It helps to have three hands.)
- If you drop a ball you lose a point. The winner is the one with the fewest drops in the time – say five minutes. (If you can't find a dead pig then use tennis balls.)

212

Knucklebones

- If your parents happen to sacrifice a sheep to the gods, ask if you can have one of its feet.
- Boil the sheep's foot until the flesh and skin fall away from the bones.
- Take the small, cubic bones and dry them. You now have five "chuck stones".
- Hold the bones in one hand. Throw them into the air. The aim is to see who can catch the most on the back of the hand.

  (Note: If your parents aren't sacrificing any sheep this week, you can use stones, dice or cubes of wood.)

Micare

- Play in pairs.
- Each player places their right hand behind their back.
- Agree on a signal – one player will nod, for example.
- On the signal, both players shoot out the right hand with a number of fingers raised.
- At the same moment each player calls out what they guess the total number of fingers will be.
- If neither guesses correctly then try again.
- The winner is the first one to guess correctly.

  (Note: This sounds easy. In fact, the more you play it, the more you learn to use clever tactics. Try it and see.)

213

The Jar Game
- Someone is selected to be "It".
- "It" sits on the ground – they are said to be "in the jar". The others try to prod or nip the one on the ground – rotten Roman children could be pretty vicious while playing this. (Warning! Only pinch or punch "It" if "It" happens to be a teacher.)
- The person in the jar cannot get up but they can try to grab hold of one of the touchers.
- The toucher who is grabbed goes into the jar.

Blind Man's Buff
- Someone is chosen to be blindfolded.
- The other players each have a stick and dance around tapping the "blind man" with the stick, shouting "Come and catch me!", which the blindfolded person tries to do.
- If a player is caught then the blindfolded person tries to guess who s/he is holding.
- If the blindfolded person is right then the caught player becomes the blindfolded one.

Nuts
- Each player has a supply of nuts – probably hazel nuts.
- Each player adds a nut to her/his pile to build a pyramid.
- The winner is the player who uses the most nuts before the pyramid collapses.
  (Note: This is a game for children. When you grew up the Romans would say you had "left your nuts". Perhaps you would like to ask your teacher, "When did you leave your nuts?")

214

Word games

If you like word-games or crosswords then you might like to make a "square" of words. They should read the same whether they are read from left to right or from top to bottom.

Here's an example from Reading in Roman Britain (now in Berkshire). It was found scratched on a tile . . .

Sator means "a sower".
Arepo is a man's name.
Tenet means "he holds".
Opera means "work" or "deeds".
Rotas means "wheels".
The square has also been translated as "The sower, Arepo, guides the wheels carefully."

BUT . . . some clever person worked out that this was not a word-game at all, but a secret, Christian prayer! Take all the letters and you can spell out the word PATERNOSTER. This is Latin for "Our Father" – the opening of the Lord's Prayer. There are two "A"s and two "O"s left over. These letters represent "the beginning and the end" to early Christians.

Clever, yes? But is it just coincidence? Or is it really a prayer? Make up your own mind.

Rotten grown-up games

The Romans enjoyed their circuses. But they weren't the sort of family day out we have at the circus today. No clowns, no jugglers, no tightrope walkers. But lots of violence, blood and death.

Augustine of Hippo wrote a book in which he told of his disgust at the bloodshed. His friend, Alypius, was taken to a Roman circus by some student friends. He set off for the circus, a real wimp. A band of trumpets played, bets were placed and the fighting began . . .

> He shut his eyes tightly, determined to have nothing to do with these horrors. If only he had closed his ears as well! The fight drew a great roar from the crowd; this thrilled him so deeply that he could not contain his curiosity. When he saw the blood it was as though he had drunk a deep cup of savage passion. Instead of turning away he fixed his eyes upon the scene and drank in all its frenzy. He revelled in the wickedness of the fighting and was drunk with the fascination of the bloodshed.

Julius Caesar, on the other hand, became a bit bored with the fighting and the dying. Long before the end of a contest he would begin reading reports and writing letters. This did *not* make him very popular with some of the spectators in the crowds!

SEEN ONE FIGHT TO THE DEATH, SEEN THEM ALL

BOO!

Gruesome gladiators – ten terrible truths

1 The Romans brought the gladiator fights to Britain ... battles between teams of armed men of whom half would be sure to lose their lives.

2 The idea of fighting and killing as a game probably began at funerals. The Roman Tertullian said ...

> Once upon a time, people believed that the souls of the dead were kept happy with human blood, and so, at funerals, they sacrificed prisoners of war or slaves of poor quality.

DO I GET A SACRIFICE AT MY FUNERAL?

These sacrifices changed into fights to the death between two men at the funeral. They became so popular that they were taken away from the funeral and put in a huge arena. The fighters became known as gladiators.

3 In Rome there had been schools of gladiators, where a slave could train and fight for a gladiator master. If he won enough battles – and murdered enough opponents – he would win a fortune and his freedom. The greatest prize was the wooden sword – a symbol of freedom.

4 Nutty Nero even ordered a battle between a woman and a dwarf as a special spectacle.

5 When a victim fell in a battle an attendant would smack him on the head with a hammer to make sure he was dead.

6 If a fighter gave up, exhausted, he could surrender. The emperor would then decide if he deserved to live or not. The crowd would usually tell him by screaming, "*Mitte!* Let him go!" or, "*Iugula!* Kill him!" The emperor would signal his decision with his thumb. Thumb down for death – thumb up for life. And we still use that sign today.

DON'T MAKE ANY QUICK DECISIONS, MULL IT OVER A WHILE, THINK ABOUT IT, TAKE YOUR TIME

7 Some of the bloodiest battles were between criminals who were under sentence of death anyway. They fought till there was no one left – an unarmed man was put in the ring with an armed man who killed him. The armed man was then disarmed and the next man killed him. And so it went on – as soon as one victim fell, another was put in the ring.

8 There's not much evidence to show that the Romans in Britain brought the sort of wild animals to the arena that they brought to Rome itself.

9 There would be bears from Scotland which were chained to a post and tormented for the entertainment of the crowd.

10 Back in Rome they would have seen . . .

- elephants against armed men – until one day, the elephants crashed through iron railings and trampled the crowd. Caesar had a moat built round the arena to protect the spectators from the animals.
- sea battles in an arena which could be flooded to take warships.
- animals fighting each other to the death – bear against buffalo, buffalo against elephant, elephant against rhinoceros.
- crocodiles, giraffes, hippopotami and ostriches – the crocodiles were tricky because they didn't survive very well when taken out of Africa. One lot spoiled the fun by refusing to eat!

- men against panthers, lions, leopards, tigers – but the men were usually heavily armed with spears, flaming torches, bows, lances and daggers. Some even took a pack of hounds into the arena to help them – they were in no more danger than the audience! One spectator made a joke about the emperor, Domitian. He was taken out of the crowd and thrown to a pack of dogs!
- men with cloaks against bulls – of the kind you can still see in Spain today.
- men fighting bears with their bare fists.
- five thousand beasts killed in one day of AD 80 in the Coliseum of Rome.

Amazing acts

But not every show in the arena was violent. Some of the acts used tame animals to perform tricks, rather as circus animals do today. The spectators were amused by . . .

- teams of tame panthers pulling chariots.
- a lion releasing a live hare from its mouth after it had caught it.
- a tiger licking the hand of its trainer.
- elephants kneeling in the sand in front of the emperor.
- elephants tracing Latin words in the sand with their trunks.

Petrifying plays

The Romans liked to visit the open-air theatres to watch plays. There were theatres in many of the bigger British towns. But if the plays were anything like the plays back in Rome, they would be banned today for being too violent!

The actors had real fights on stage. Then, Emperor Domitian allowed a real death on the stage. At the end of the play "Laureolis" the villain has to be crucified, tortured and torn apart by a bear. The actor playing the villain left the stage and his place was taken by a criminal who was under the sentence of death. The really rotten Romans enjoyed watching this horrible spectacle.

Then, of course, the Romans used the theatres as an excuse to execute people they didn't like – they put men, women and children in with wild animals, sometimes just for the simple crime of being Christians.

Strangely, it was the Christian religion that finally put an end to the massacres. When the emperors became Christian they banned the bloodthirsty events. On 1 October 326 AD, Emperor Constantine put a stop to the gladiator schools and, by the end of the century, the shows had disappeared from the empire.

Did you know?

The term "Roman Holiday" is still used to describe people enjoying themselves by watching others suffering. So, when teachers try to tell you the Romans "civilised" the Ancient Britons, you can tell them that the rotten Romans had some of the most "uncivilised" fun and games in history.

221

ROTTEN ROMAN FOOD

The Romans introduced new foods to Britain, and new recipes. They'd travelled the world and weren't too keen to eat the coarse bread or drink the ale of the Britons. They could afford spices to disguise the boring taste of the smoked or salted meat and fish.

Twenty foul food facts

1 The rich had great feasts. One Roman, called Trimalchio, held a feast which included wine that was a hundred years old. It also included a wild boar that, when sliced down the belly, allowed song-thrushes to fly out.

2 During such feasts the guests could eat so much that they had to be sick; a special room was set aside for them called a vomitorium. They would then go back into the dining room to continue eating!

3 Emperor Maximian was a big eater. He was supposed to have eaten 20 kilograms of meat a day . . . that's about all the meat you'd get from a small sheep!

4 Maximian also enjoyed about 34 litres of wine each day. Such gluttony killed him in the end, of course . . . but not until he'd reigned almost 20 years!

5 In the kitchen, the rich kept a special container used for fattening up their dormice. They were fed on the very best food – walnuts, acorns and chestnuts, before being killed, stuffed and served as a great delicacy. The stuffing could be made from pork sausage (or even sausage made from other dormice) and flavoured with pepper and nuts.

6 Snails fattened in milk were popular. Take your live snails out of their shells and put them in a shallow dish of milk and salt for a day. They love milk so they slurp it down, but the salt just makes the stupid creatures thirstier! Then they are placed in plain milk for a few days. They drink and drink till they become too fat to get back in their shells. Fried in oil and served covered in wine sauce – they are delicious!

7 Even fouler . . . fatten up the snails on raw flesh to add to their flavour. (Most snails would be vampire snails given the chance!)

223

8 The Romans enjoyed stuffed thrush. No worse than your Sunday chicken, right? Wrong! They stuffed the thrush through the throat without taking the insides out! Yeuch! The Romans also ate other birds that we wouldn't usually think of eating. They enjoyed . . .

- herring-gulls
- jackdaws
- crows
- ravens
- swans
- coots
- peacocks

9 The Romans didn't waste much. One recipe by Apicius calls for the chopped-up udder of a sow. They also ate the brains of animals . . . not to mention the lungs of goats and sheep.

10 King Mithradates of Pontus in Asia was scared of being poisoned, so he ate . . . poison! In small doses, of course. That way his body built up a resistance to poison. Then he heard the Romans were coming to get him and he hadn't the guts to face them. So he swallowed poison. Of course, it didn't work! He had to fall on his sword in the end. (So, when the Romans found him he had even less guts!)

THIS JUST ISN'T MY DAY

11 The Romans had some rotten drinks, too. One was made from the guts of fish. They were salted and left to rot in the sun. After a few days the liquid was drained off and drunk or used as a sauce – the way you may sprinkle tomato ketchup on your chips. (This may sound a fishy story, but it's true!)

12 The Romans ate chicken, duck and goose, just as we still do. But the Romans probably served them at the table with the heads cut off but the feet still on!

13 In Roman times there were storks living in Britain. The Romans ate those too. (Could you tell stork from mutton?)

14 Horse bones have been found at Verulamium, which shows that the Romans ate horse-meat sausages. (Neigh! It's true!)

15 For vegetables, the Romans used some pretty odd things. Would you have eaten a salad made with dandelion leaves? How about an egg custard made with nettles? Or perhaps you'd prefer some stewed seaweed? These things are still eaten today in various parts of the world.

16 Sometimes, Roman banquet guests would drop rose petals into their wine.

17 At one meal, Heliogabalus served his guests 600 ostrich brains.

18 He also served peas mixed with grains of gold, and lentils mixed with precious stones – perhaps they liked rich food!

19 A favourite game was to disguise food so that it looked like something it wasn't! At one feast, roast piglets turned out to be made of pastry. At another, a nest seemed to be filled with eggs – but the eggs were made of pastry and inside, the "yolks" were made of spiced garden-warbler meat.

20 You might enjoy a meal while watching television. But could you eat at a Roman feast with dancers and acrobats, jugglers and clowns rushing around? Or even a pair of gladiators trying to kill each other?

The rotten Romans' daily diet

The main meals of the day for the Romans in Britain were:

MENU

BREAKFAST
BREAD AND FRUIT

LUNCH (PRANDIUM)
COLD EGGS, FISH OR VEGETABLES

DINNER (CENA)
GUSTATIO – TASTY THINGS LIKE RADISHES OR ASPARAGUS AS A STARTER.
PRIMAE MENSALA – THE MAIN COURSE ; CHICKEN OR HARE AND FISH AND VEGETABLE DISHES.
SECUNDAE MENSAE – SWEET COURSE , INCLUDING FRUIT

Rotten Roman beastly banquet

Why not invite your friends to a Roman-style banquet. Or, even better, invite your enemies.

First get your slaves to lay the table with napkins for each guest, a spoon and a knife. No forks, you will notice. If you want to try a Roman banquet then you'll have to eat with your fingers and have a napkin to keep your fingers clean! For the soft food and sauces you can use a spoon, and a knife for cutting or spearing meat.

Before you start, place some of your food in a small bowl in front of the statue of the family god. (If the god doesn't eat it then the slaves will!)

226

Say a few prayers. The Romans would say, *"Auguste, patri patriae"* – "Good luck to the emperor, father of our country."

Have your slaves wash and dry the feet of your guests. (If you can't find any slaves at the local supermarket or corner shop then you could always use a parent or teacher.)

Warning: Do not cook this food yourself! Have it done for you by your slaves!

Starter *(Gustatio)*

If your local shop doesn't have stuffed dormice or snails fattened in milk, then you may like to try shellfish, hard-boiled eggs or a dish of olives. Serve with spiced wine – or in your case, grape juice!

SPICED WINE

INGREDIENTS:
- 1 LITRE OF GRAPE JUICE
- 3 TABLESPOONS OF HONEY
- MIXED SPICE
- CINNAMON
- NUTMEG
- BLACK PEPPER
- WATER

METHOD:
- POUR GRAPE JUICE INTO A 2 LITRE SERVING JUG
- ADD A LITRE OF WATER – LESS IF YOU LIKE YOUR WINE STRONG
- STIR IN THE HONEY TILL IT DISSOLVES
- ADD A PINCH OF MIXED SPICE, ONE OF NUTMEG, CINNAMON AND BLACK PEPPER.
- TASTE IT AND ADD MORE HONEY IF IT'S NOT SWEET ENOUGH OR SPICES IF YOU WANT IT TASTIER.

NUMIDIAN CHICKEN

INGREDIENTS:

- CHICKEN PIECES (1 FOR EACH PERSON)
- CUMIN POWDER (QUARTER TEASPOON)
- CORIANDER SEEDS (QUARTER TEASPOON)
- 4 DATES (CHOPPED INTO SMALL PIECES)
- CHOPPED NUTS (4 TABLESPOONS)
- HONEY (2 TABLESPOONS)
- WINE VINEGAR (2 TABLESPOONS)
- CHICKEN STOCK (1 CHICKEN STOCK CUBE CRUMBLED IN A CUP OF WATER)
- PEPPER (A PINCH)
- COOKING OIL (1 TABLESPOON)
- BREAD CRUMBS (1 SLICE OF DRY BREAD)

METHOD:

- PUT THE CHICKEN PIECES IN A ROASTING DISH. BRUSH THEM WITH COOKING OIL, SPRINKLE THEM WITH PEPPER AND COVER THE DISH WITH COOKING FOIL. ROAST THE PIECES AT 350°F, 180°C OR GAS MARK 4 FOR HALF AN HOUR.
- WHILE THE CHICKEN IS ROASTING, PUT THE OTHER INGREDIENTS INTO A PAN AND SIMMER FOR TWENTY MINUTES TO MAKE NUMIDIAN SAUCE.
- WHEN THE CHICKEN PIECES ARE READY, PUT THEM ON A SERVING DISH AND POUR OVER THE SAUCE
- SERVE THE CHICKEN WITH VEGETABLES – CABBAGES AND BEANS ARE VERY ROMAN.

DATES COOKED IN HONEY

INGREDIENTS:

- 12 FRESH DATES*
- 12 HALF WALNUTS
- 4 TABLESPOONS HONEY
- SALT
- BLACK PEPPER

(*IF YOU CAN'T GET FRESH DATES THEN A PACKET OF COOKING DATES WILL DO)

METHOD:

- PEEL THE DATES AND TAKE OUT THE STONES
- REPLACE EACH STONE WITH A HALF WALNUT
- SPRINKLE EACH DATE LIGHTLY WITH SALT
- MELT THE HONEY IN A PAN AND GENTLY COOK THE DATES *IN THE HONEY*
- AFTER COOKING FOR FIVE MINUTES, TAKE OUT THE DATES AND ARRANGE ON A SERVING DISH
- SPOON MORE HONEY OVER THE HOT DATES
- SPRINKLE ON A LITTLE BLACK PEPPER AND SERVE

Finish off with fruit and nuts and grape-juice wine. While eating your meal, have some entertainment from jugglers, dancers, singers or musicians.

It isn't polite to talk too much at a Roman banquet. But if you must talk, then don't chatter about common things – football, fashion or the neighbour's new car – talk about important things like life, death and great teachers of our time.

Rotten Roman remedies

It didn't do to be sick in Roman times. Sometimes the cure was worse than the illness! Here's a letter from a Roman, Cassius, to his sister, Juliet. Would you like to try some of his cures . . .?

DEAREST JULIET
 I HAVE BEEN VERY WORRIED EVER SINCE I GOT YOUR LETTER TELLING ME THAT YOR WERE BITTEN BY A SPIDER HIDDEN AMONG THE VEGETABLES FROM THE GARDEN. IN APULIA THERE ARE A LOT OF DANGEROUS SPIDERS CALLED TARANTULAS. THE BEST REMEDY FOR THEIR BITE IS, AS YOU KNOW, TO CRUSH THE BODY OF THE SPIDER ON THE WOUND. IF THAT IS IMPOSSIBLE THEN COVER THE SPOT WITH A PIECE OF ITS WEB.
 ALTHOUGH YOU TELL ME YOU ARE BETTER I ADVISE YOU TO COME TO ROME AS SOON AS YOU CAN. WE WILL GO TOGETHER TO MAKE A SACRIFICE AT THE TEMPLE OF THE GODDESS CYBELE.
 THERE ARE ALSO SOME USEFUL REMEDIES USING FROGS AS INGREDIENTS. A BROTH MADE OF SHRIMPS, FLOUR AND FROGS, BOILED IN WINE IS EXCELLENT FOR ANYONE WHO HAS LOST WEIGHT AND IS SUFFERING FROM TIREDNESS. CRUSHED FROGS, SOAKED IN WINE, ARE GOOD AGAINST THE POISONING OF TOADS.
 FINALLY, TO CURE THE KIND OF FEVER WHICH COMES AROUND EVERY FOUR DAYS, YOU SHOULD EAT THE FLESH OF FROGS COOKED IN OLIVE OIL.
 GIVE MY GREETINGS TO YOUR HUSBAND AND MY GOOD WISHES TO YOURSELF
 YOUR LOVING BROTHER,

CASSIUS

ROTTEN ROMAN RELIGIONS

The Romans brought their religion and their gods with them from Rome, though in time they became mixed with the native British religions.

Lucky charms and cruel curses

In the Roman home the Lares were very important. These were household gods. They protected the home from evil spirits. In richer homes, Romans would also worship gods like . . .

Vesta – goddess of the fire and hearth . . . and you can still buy matches called "Vestas"!

Penates – guardian of the store cupboard . . . made sure nobody sneaked any midnight feasts.

Janus – the two-faced god who used his two faces to watch the people coming into the house and those going out.

The hot spring waters in the city of Bath are used as cures for all sorts of illnesses by people today. They were used by the Romans too. The Romans were a bit superstitious and believed there was magic in the water. They threw things into the water to take advantage of its powers. They threw coins in – probably as you would into a wishing well – 12,000 Roman coins have been found there.

They also threw in written tablets, usually trying to make a deal with a god – "You do this for me, god, and I'll build an altar for you, OK?" Many of these requests were for curses – if the name of the person you wanted to curse was written backwards, then the magic would be even stronger.

One man lost his girlfriend, Vilbia, to another man. He scratched the curse on a piece of metal . . . but wrote it backwards. Then he threw it in the water where it was found hundreds of years later. It read . . .

retaw ekil diuqil otni nrut ot em morf aibliV
koot ohw nosrep eht tnaw I

(Do you know anyone you'd like to turn into a real drip?)

An even nastier curse has been found in Clothall. It was nailed onto some object, perhaps a dead animal, and says . . .

Tacita is cursed by this and will be decayed like rotting blood.

The waters of Bath weren't just used for cursing. The waters were famous for healing long before the Romans came to Britain . . .

The story of Bladud

BLADUD WAS THE SON OF A KING OF THE BRITONS

THAT'S MY LAD BLAD!

BUT BLADUD BECAME ILL WITH LEPROSY, HE HAD TO LEAVE HOME

THAT'S SAD BLAD

BYE... DAD

HIS MOTHER GAVE HIM A RING

COME BACK WHEN YOU'RE NOT SO BAD BLAD

HE LEFT AND FOUND A JOB AS A PIG KEEPER

I ONCE WORE ROBES BUT NOW I'M A POORLY CLAD BLAD

OINK

BUT TRAGEDY STRUCK! THE PIGS CAUGHT LEPROSY FROM BLAD!

WORST ITCH I'VE EVER HAD, BLAD!

THE ITCHING DROVE THE PIGS WILD, THEY RAN DOWN THE HILL AND INTO AN OOZING, BLACK BOG

I'M GOING MAD, BLAD!

Nasty native religions

1 The Celts believed that gods and spirits were present in all natural things.

2 Their priests were known as Druids. The Druids were local judges as well as priests. If they sentenced you to be kept out of the temple, then no one would want to speak to you.

3 Most of the religious ceremonies were held in woods – especially oak woods where there were magical mistletoe plants.

4 At first the Romans allowed the Celtic religion to continue alongside their own. They even allowed the Druids to build temples similar to the Roman ones.

5 After a while they began to suspect the Druids of leading the rebellions against Roman rule. Most of the Druids were put to death.

6 The Celtic heaven was like earth – only better! There was no old age or sickness and everyone was beautiful. The sun always shone, the birds always sang and there was always plenty to eat and drink. Food appeared as if by magic whenever you felt like it.

7 Death and heaven were so good that the warriors were quite keen to get there! That's why they were so fearless in battle . . . they didn't mind dying.

8 The one thing that the Celtic warrior feared was the sky falling down! That's what would happen if the gods were upset.

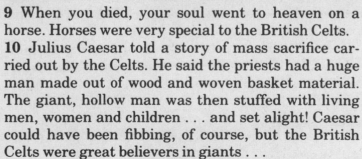

9 When you died, your soul went to heaven on a horse. Horses were very special to the British Celts.

10 Julius Caesar told a story of mass sacrifice carried out by the Celts. He said the priests had a huge man made out of wood and woven basket material. The giant, hollow man was then stuffed with living men, women and children . . . and set alight! Caesar could have been fibbing, of course, but the British Celts were great believers in giants . . .

235

The History of Britain . . . by a mad monk!

In the 12th century, Geoffrey of Monmouth told the story of Britain. It was not the history that you will read here and it's not the history your teachers will tell you! But we could be wrong and Geoffrey could be right. What do you think? Here's Geoffrey's history . . .

After the Trojan War – you know, the one where the siege of Troy was ended with the trick of the wooden horse – Brutus and his Trojan warriors came to Britain. Of course, the Trojan War was in the 13th century BC . . . before Rome was even thought of.

Brutus found that the British Isles were inhabited by giants. Brutus gave General Corineus the job of conquering Cornwall. Corineus killed the giants and was left with just one final giant – Gogmagog. Corineus wrestled with the four-metre man and threw him to his death in the sea. That's how Britain came to be free of giants!

Believe that, do you? Or is it just a TALL story? Old Geoffrey believed it. And so did many Britons, probably.

The Britons had their own stories and many were stories of heroes fighting giants. Some of the stories are still told today. But, because children are easily scared, most story-tellers miss out the gory bits.

Here's an old British folk-tale with the gory bits put back in. If you suffer from nightmares *don't read it* . . . or read it with your eyes shut. You have been warned!

A bloody British tale

Once upon a long-ago time in Cornwall, there lived the giant, Cormoran, with his wife, Cormelian.

Cormoran was big and Cormoran was a bully. "I want a castle and I want it built of white granite!" he told his wife.

"That'll be nice, dear," his wife nodded. "But there's no white granite round here. Only green granite. You'll have ever so far to carry it!"

"I won't carry it," Cormoran sneered. "You will!"

"Will I?" Cormelian blinked. "Why?"

"Because I'm telling you to," the cruel man cackled. "Now, get started!"

Cormelian trudged off to find the white granite and struggled to carry it back. Even though every step took her six miles it was hard and heavy work. When she returned the third time she saw that Cormoran was asleep.

"I'll just fetch a few loads of the green granite," the giant's wife sighed. "He'll never notice!"

But, as she brought the load of green stone, Cormoran woke up. "What's this?" he roared and gave her such a kick that her apron strings snapped. The stones tumbled down and sank Mount's Bay forest into the sea and drowned the people.

"Now look what you made me do!" Cormelian grumbled, rubbing her sore bum. She went off in a huff.

Cormoran piled the white granite into a castle – you can see it today in Cornwall. It's known as St Michael's Mount. The huge green stone that Cormelian dropped can be seen on the road to the mount.

Anyway, the poor people were horrified by the sinking of the forest. "Whatever shall we do?" they cried. "Mount's Bay forest has gone today – we'll be next!"

Just then, along came the local hero, Jack. Jack the giant-killer. Jack had killed giants by digging deep pits in the ground. When the giants fell in, their heads came up to the level of Jack. A quick whack with his axe would split the giants' skulls and kill them with a single blow. The pit became their gruesome, brain-spattered grave.

This time Jack had another plan.

First he collected as much food as he could find and placed it at the foot of St Michael's Mount.

Then he made a special coat with a huge pouch in the front.

Lastly he blew his horn to wake up the giant Cormoran. The angry giant glared at Jack. "What do you want, shorty?"

"I want to challenge you to an eating competition," the hero announced.

BREAKFAST?

"No problem," the giant shrugged and sat down to stuff himself with a pile of food. Jack pretended to eat, but really slipped the food into the pouch in the front of his coat.

The giant began to slow down. At last he stopped. Jack nibbled at a roast cow. "Give in?" he asked cheerfully.

"Certainly not!" Cormoran roared. "But I'd like to know where you're putting all that food."

Jack shrugged. "In my stomach," he said, patting the front of his pouch. "In fact, I can empty my stomach and start again. Then I'm bound to win!"

"How?" the stupid giant asked.

Jack took a dagger from his belt. He placed it at one side of his pouch and dragged it across. The pouch split open and the food tumbled out. "Easy!"

"Hah! Two can play at that game," Cormoran sniffed. He took out his knife, stuck it in his fat belly and dragged it across. "Ouch!" he cried as the food tumbled out . . . and most of his guts. "Ooooh!" he sobbed. "I think I've just killed meself!"

And he had.

A bloody end

An equally nasty story tells of the equally stupid giant, Bolster, who fell in love with the beautiful St Agnes. She asked him to prove his love by filling a hole in the ground with his blood. He agreed and opened a vein. He didn't know that the hole led to a cave that led out to the sea. Bolster bled for hours and died in the end. There's a hole at Chapel Porth in Cornwall, and red stains mark the rocks around!

239

The rottenest Roman religions

Chucking chickens

The Roman Army had its own religions and its own superstitions. The General of an army would look at the liver of certain animals for signs as to how a battle might go. They might also . . .

- observe the flight of birds – the ways in which crows flew, for example.
- observe the way the sacred chickens ate their food – Claudius Pulcher took chickens with him on a voyage to the Punic wars. The chickens were probably a bit seasick, because they refused to eat at all – a bad sign. So Claudius Pulcher ordered them to be thrown overboard with the words, "If they won't eat then let them drink!" He went on to lose the battle and the soldiers blamed him for drowning the sacred chickens!

I'M FEELING A LOT HUNGRIER NOW!

Stomach signals

A Roman teacher, Fronto, wrote to his pupil, Marcus, with news that he had a pain in the stomach. He believed this was a sign from the gods that there was bad luck coming to his family. (If your teacher had a pain in the stomach, she'd be more likely to blame school dinners!)

240

Mighty Mithras

The religion of the bull-god Mithras, was very popular with many Roman soldiers. He was probably brought to Britain by the legionaries who served in Persia, where Mithras was a popular god.

Mithras was the "judge" of the afterlife – he decided who should go to heaven and who should go to hell after they died.

The temples of Mithras were dark and gloomy places – sometimes underground – and a lot of the soldiers must have enjoyed joining this religion, because it was like joining a secret society.

You couldn't enter the temples until you'd performed certain brave deeds – like allowing yourself to be locked up for several hours in a coffin! The base of the coffin was on the stone-cold floor and the side was close to a fire – you froze and fried at the same time!

Bull's blood

Another Eastern "mystery" religion had equally gruesome rituals, as Prudentius described in the 4th century AD . . .

241

> The worshippers dig a deep pit and the High Priest is lowered into it. Above him they put a platform of loose planks. Each plank has tiny holes drilled in it. A huge bull is stood on the platform. They take a sacred hunting spear and drive it into the bull's heart. The hot blood spurts out of the deep wound. It falls through the holes in the planks like rotten rain onto the priest below. His clothes and body are covered in the animal's gore. Afterwards he climbs out of the pit. It is a dreadful sight to see.

Christianity

From the end of the first century AD, Christianity began to enter Britain. After the exciting Roman religions some Christians seemed a bit boring. One Christian writer, Tertullian, was against fancy clothes – he didn't even like to see them dyed. He wrote . . .

> If God had wanted us to wear purple and sky-blue clothes, then He would have given us purple and sky-blue sheep!

PURPLE? WITH ALL THIS GREEN GRASS AROUND? WE'D CLASH!

242

By 250 AD, the emperors began stamping out Christianity and killing Christians. St Alban was one of the victims in Britain. Still, Christianity continued to grow there.

Then, in 313 AD, the Act of Toleration was passed that allowed Christians to worship openly. But it was all too late for poor old Alban . . .

The legend of St Alban

The wind blew wild and wet along the wall. Two soldiers shivered behind their shields and complained.

"End of the world, this place. End of the world!" old Laganus groaned.

"Not quite the end of the world," his young partner pointed out. "There are people on the other side of the wall!"

"People!" Laganus laughed. "Them Picts aren't *people!* More what you'd call *animals.* Proper people wouldn't live out in that wild country. They're *savages,* Paul, *savages!*"

Young Paul huddled into his cloak and looked across the bleak and empty moors. "Not as savage as the Romans can be," he said carefully.

"That's no way to talk about our masters!" Laganus gasped. "That's the sort of talk that'll get you beaten!"

Paul nodded. "That's what I mean. They'll beat me. They're cruel."

The older man snorted. "You're just soft, my boy. You've got to kill your enemy. Kill or get yourself killed. That's the way it is!"

"You wouldn't say that if you were a Christian," Paul told him.

Laganus turned on him savagely. "Yeh! I've heard

all about your Christian God! Look at that Alban!"

"They killed him!" Paul cried. "The Romans killed him!"

"But that's nothing to what your kind and gentle God did for revenge, is it?" the old soldier sneered. He sat down in the shelter of the wall and rubbed his freezing hands. "I heard the true story from a soldier of the Seventh Legion last week."

Paul crouched down beside him. "Alban was a hero. A Christian martyr . . ."

"Alban was a soldier just like you or me. Well, more like *you*, Paul. He was soft-hearted. Soft in the head too, if you ask me. The Romans were having one of their crackdowns on the Christians. You know the sort of thing. Killing a few here and there to show them who is boss."

"Murder," Paul muttered.

"Alban was a *Roman* soldier, of course. He should have been joining in the *killing* of the Christians. Instead he gave *shelter* to a Christian priest."

"Amphibalus," the young soldier nodded.

"And worse! He let this Amphibalus talk *him* into becoming a Christian!" Laganus groaned. "They sent soldiers to arrest Alban, of course. What did he do? Disguised himself and tried to run away."

"They caught him," Paul sighed.

"Of course they caught him! But they didn't kill him for hiding the enemy – they didn't kill him for becoming a Christian . . ."

"They did!" Paul cut in.

"No, no, no! They gave him a chance. They told him to make a sacrifice to the Roman gods. Prove that he was still loyal!" the old soldier said.

"He refused."

"So it serves him right if he was sentenced to

244

death," Laganus snorted. "But the Romans didn't have him tortured or crucified or stoned to death. No. They were kind. They sentenced him to a quick death by beheading!"

"They murdered him," Paul repeated stubbornly.

"Ah, but that was quick and kind. What happened at the execution, eh? You Christians never tell about that!"

The young soldier shrugged. "I don't know."

Laganus grinned. "Two soldiers led Alban to the place of execution. Alban managed to convert one of them on the way. But he didn't convert the second one, did he? The second executioner cut off Alban's head! *Then* your 'kind', kind God took his cruel, cruel revenge. As Alban's head hit the ground the executioner staggered back clutching his face. When the guards reached him they found that his eyes had both dropped out! Plop! Plop!"

By the end of that century, Christianity became the religion of the Roman State. But some parts of the British Isles were converted as the result of a strange accident . . .

Pirates, pagans and Patrick –
Did you know?

1 Patrick is the patron saint of Ireland, BUT he was born in Wales, lived in England and his parents were Roman.

2 When he was 16 he was kidnapped by Celtic pirates and taken as a slave to Ireland.

3 He was given a rotten job by the Irish pagans. Looking after cattle on the bleak hills.

4 A boulder crashed down the mountainside towards Patrick. Just before it flattened him it split in two. One piece went on either side of him.

5 Patrick took this as a miracle. He believed it was a sign from God that there was special work for him.

6 He escaped to Gaul, then returned home to become a farmer. He still felt that his life had been saved for some special reason.

7 He boldly went back to Ireland.

8 He performed miracles there. There is a story, for example, that there are no snakes in Ireland because Patrick got rid of them all.

9 Patrick converted the kings of many Irish kingdoms to Christianity. The kings were baptised and the people followed the kings.

10 A king of southern Ireland had a rotten baptism. Patrick carried a crook – like a shepherd. It was pointed on the bottom. During the baptism Patrick accidentally put the point clean through the king's foot. The king didn't complain; he thought it was all part of the ceremony.

ROTTEN ROMAN FACTS

The rottenest Roman historian

At the eastern end of the Roman Wall is a fort. In 1971 the museum at the fort proudly showed their latest find. "It is a sestertius coin, made between 135 AD and 138 AD. On the back of the coin is a large letter 'R' – standing for Roma," they said.

Then an expert, Miss Fiona Gordon, told them they were wrong. The sestertius was, in fact, a free gift given away with bottles of fruit squash. "The letter 'R' stands for the name of the makers, Robinson!"

The museum keepers discovered Miss Gordon was correct. That was embarrassing! But, most embarrassing of all, Miss Fiona Gordon was just nine years old!

True or false?

1 A favourite method of execution in ancient Rome was "stinging to death".
2 The Roman Fort at Sinodum is supposed to be the site of a money-pit full of buried treasure.
3 Druids picked their victims by going "Eeny-meeny-miney-mo . . ."

REMIND ME, WHAT COMES AFTER MO?

4 Women could be Druids.

5 Druids would stab a victim in the back, then see the future from the way he died.

6 A crash at a chariot race was called "a plane-crash".

7 The Victorians pulled down the east end of Hadrian's Wall and used the stone to mend their roads.

8 The Romans didn't have peppermint toothpaste. They preferred powdered mouse-brains.

9 The Romans stopped traffic jams in Aldborough by building a bypass.

THIS ONE I'LL CALL A FLYOVER

10 In Roman horse races the losing horse was killed.

Answers:

1 True – the victim was smothered in honey then covered with angry wasps.

2 True – in the 19th century a local villager was digging at the fort one day when he came across an iron chest. A raven landed on it and said, "He is not born yet!" The villager thought this meant, "The person who can open the chest is not yet born." He filled the hole in and left. Are you the one born to open the chest?

3 True – according to Victorian experts. The shepherds of ancient Britain would count sheep with a number system that sounded very like "Eeny-meeny-miney-mo". The Druids could well have used it. Children may then have copied it as part of a gruesome game and it's been used in children's games ever since.

4 True – the Romans said that they met Druidesses. These women were good at telling fortunes.

5 True – the Roman historian, Strabo, said the way a man twisted and fell after he had been stabbed helped a Druid to read the fortunes for his tribe.

6 False – it was called a "shipwreck".

7 True. There are still large stretches of Hadrian's wall to be seen across the North of England. It's well looked after now . . . but it hasn't always been. Farmers pinched stones from the Wall to build their houses, and the Victorians were worse. They pulled the wall down, smashed up the stones into little bits and used them to repair the roads of Newcastle!

8 True – perhaps they wanted their teeth to be "squeaky" clean! They also used powdered horn, oyster-shell ash and the ashes of dogs' teeth mixed with honey.

9 True.

10 False – the *winning* horse was killed as a sacrifice to the god of war, Mars. The local people often fought fiercely to decide who would have the honour of sticking its head on their wall.

Rotten Roman towns

Everyone tells you about how marvellous the Roman baths were. But not *all* of the Romans were so keen. One Roman wrote . . .

> *I live above the public baths, and we all know what that means. Yeuch! It's sickening. Firstly there are the strong men doing exercises, swinging lead weights round with grunts and . . .*

. . . groans. Then there are the lazy ones having a cheap massage – I can hear them being slapped on the back. Then there are the noises of fighters and thieves being arrested. Worst is the sound of the man who likes to hear his own voice in the bath. And what about the ones who leap into the bath and make a huge splash in the water?

Rotten Romans today

The Rotten Romans ran the world for a long time. There are still signs of their life today.

Did you know?

1 The Romans signed their "trademark" wherever they went. They wrote the letters SPQR, which stood for Senatus Populus Que Romanus – The Senate and the People of Rome. The buses and the drain covers of Rome have the letters on them today.

2 The Roman language is called Latin. It is still used in some religious ceremonies and used to be taught in many schools. But no one speaks it as an everyday language now. So it's called a "dead" language. That's why schoolchildren who still have to learn it mutter the same old school chant . . .

LATIN IS A LANGUAGE
AS DEAD AS DEAD CAN BE
IT KILLED THE ANCIENT BRITONS-
AND NOW IT'S KILLING ME!

3 Much of the Roman Wall can still be seen – and walked along – in the north of England. But the famous historian and monk, St Bede, got his facts about Hadrian's wall completely wrong! He said the Romans built it just before they abandoned Britain. It was a sort of farewell present for the Britons, planned to keep the Picts and Scots out. He wrote . . .

> *When the Wall was finished, the Romans gave clear advice to the dejected Britons, then said goodbye to their friends and never returned. The gloomy British soldiers lived in terror day and night. Beyond the Wall the enemy constantly attacked them with hooked weapons, dragging the defenders down from the Wall and dashing them to the ground. At last the Britons abandoned their cities and the Wall and fled in confusion.*

Wrong! The Wall was there 300 years before the Romans left. Don't believe everything you read in history books – even if the writer is a saint!

4 There are some rotten things in Britain today that we can blame the Romans for. They brought them here. Things like . . .

- **stinging nettles** – next time you sit on one, you can cry out in agony, "Oooh! The rotten Romans!"
- **cabbages and peas** – the sort of vegetables your parents make you eat because "they're good for you." Next time you hear that, you can say, "The Ancient Britons survived a few million years without them!"

252

- **cats** – yes, blame the Romans for that mangy moggy that yowls all night on the corner of your street and keeps you awake. When teacher tells you off for yawning in class, say, "Don't blame me – blame the rotten Romans!"

5 Rotten spelling – a lot of the words we use today come from Latin. They made sense to the Rotten Romans but they don't make sense to us. Take the Latin word "plumbum". . . . no, it doesn't mean purple bottom. It means waterworks. So we get a word for a man who fixes your leaky waterworks from that. That's right, "plumber". We say it "plummer" and any sensible Briton in their right mind would spell it "plummer". But the Romans put that useless "b" in the middle, so we have to. Next time you get two out of ten for your spelling test say, "Don't blame me – blame the rotten Romans!"

6 False teeth – the Romans generally had good teeth. They cleaned them regularly and didn't have sugar to rot them. But, if they did lose a tooth, they used false teeth. These would be made of gold or ivory. They'd be held in place with gold wire. That wire could also be used to hold loose teeth in place. The poor people just had to let them drop out.

Ancient Roman Ancient Joke:

DOCTOR DOCTOR! HAVE YOU GOT SOMETHING TO KEEP MY TEETH IN?

CERTAINLY, MADAM, HERE'S A PAPER BAG!

7 Skyscrapers – the Romans made buildings with more floors than anyone else of their age. But this led to some rotten Roman tragedies. In 217 BC an ox escaped from the local market. It ran into a three-storey building and up the stairs. When it reached the top it threw itself out of a window on the top floor. By the time of Augustus the crowded cities were forcing people to build houses higher and higher – a bit like Britain in the 1960s! But many of these tower blocks began to collapse – so Augustus passed a law banning any building over 20 metres tall.

8 A family living in Hertford, England, are so keen on the Romans that they eat Roman food (like sardines stuffed with dates – yeuch!) and play Roman games after dinner. The family have organised a new Fourteenth Legion (but with only 24 legionaries so far) who go on 40-kilometre marches just as the original legion did. They also dress as Romans occasionally and go around schools to give demonstrations to children. This does not always have the desired result – sometimes younger pupils see the Roman soldier walk into the classroom and they burst into tears . . . usually the boys! Oh, and the daughter of the family isn't a fan of the Romans and is too embarrassed by her Roman family to bring her boyfriend home!

9 We have Christmas traditions today that live on from Roman times. One tradition is Roman and one British. They were . . .

● **holly** – The Romans had ceremonies for their god, Saturn, in December. The decoration they used was holly. Country people still believe that it's a protection against poison, storms, fire and "the evil eye".

- **mistletoe** – trees were sacred to the Britons. Mistletoe grew on trees and sucked the spirit from them – that's the sticky juice in the berries. The oak was the *most* sacred tree, so mistletoe from the oak was the most precious plant of all. Druids in white robes cut it with golden knives on the sixth day of a new moon. A sprig over the door protected the house from thunder, lightning and all evil.

OUR MISTLETOE MUST HAVE GONE OFF

10 Christianity put an end to the Druids' human sacrifices . . . but 2000 years later we may still have curious memories of those deadly days . . . the children's game *London Bridge is Falling Down.* Some form of this game is known all over the world.

Two children link hands and form an arch. The rest of the children have to pass under the arch while chanting the song. When a child is caught, then the bridge has fallen. That child becomes the "watchman" of the bridge.

But the legends say that, in the days of pagan beliefs, the unlucky child could only guard the bridge if he (or she) was dead! It seems the spirits of rivers hate bridges and without a sacrifice they would bring it down. The British legend says that children were sacrificed and their blood poured over the stones of the first London Bridge to keep "Old Father Thames" happy.

255

EPILOGUE

The Romans left to defend their homeland and Rome. The Britons were left to defend the island against enemies old and new. A historian from those times, Gildas, described how the "foul" Picts and Scots with their "lust for blood" swarmed over Hadrian's mighty Wall. They pulled the British defenders down from the Wall and killed them like "lambs are slaughtered by butchers". The men from the north with their hairy "hang-dog" faces took over.

Four hundred years before, the Britons had fought the Romans off. But in four hundred years the Britons had forgotten how to fight. Suddenly the Romans didn't seem so rotten after all. Now the Britons wrote and begged them to return . . .

The barbarians drive us to the sea, the sea drives us back to the barbarians. Between these two methods of death we are either massacred or drowned.

But no help came. Rome had problems of its own. After hundreds of years of Roman rule, Britain entered "The Dark Ages".

256